Seen through the potter's eyes, the truth God placed in His Word centuries ago comes alive as we catch a glimmer of what it means for God to search out His clay, refine it, shape it, and set it forth for His use.

Worthy Vessels personalizes God and personifies us, His clay.

Photo by Gillian E. Shaw

Nell L. Kennedy is a photojournalist, reporter, correspondent, and Bible teacher who has lived and worked in Japan for sixteen years. Her articles have appeared in numerous periodicals and she is the author of *Dream Your Way to Success,* the authorized biography of Dr. Yonggi Cho.

"I began to understand the limitations of the clay and why some clays crack under stress and some turn into beautiful pottery. However, I came closest to understanding the heart of God one day when one of the potters opened his kiln after months of tedious work, only to find that every vessel had warped or cracked except one tiny cup which he picked up and held quietly in his hands. And he stood at the gaping kiln and cried."

WORTHY VESSELS

WORTHY VESSELS

Clay in the Hands of the Master Potter

WORTHY VESSELS

*Clay in the Hands
of the Master Potter*

Nell L. Kennedy

Guideposts

CARMEL • NEW YORK 10512

This Guideposts edition is published by
special arrangement with Zondervan Corporation.

ZONDERVAN BOOKS are published by
Zondervan Publishing House, 1415 Lake Drive, S.E.
Grand Rapids, Michigan 49506

Unless otherwise indicated,
Scripture verses quoted in this book
are taken from the *New International
Version of the Bible,*© 1978 by
the New York International Bible Society.
Used by permission of Zondervan Bible Publishers.

Library of Congress Cataloging in Publication Data

Kennedy, Nell L.
  Worthy vessels.

  Bibliography: p.
  1. Christian life—1960–   . 2. Potters. I. Title.
BV4501.2.K433   1984   248.4   84-25826
ISBN 0-310-47100-1

*Photographs by Nell L. Kennedy
Designed by Judith E. Markham and Martha Bentley
Edited by Linda VanderZalm and Judith E. Markham*

Printed in the United States of America

85 86 87 88 89 90 / 8 7 6 5 4 3 2 1

To the Potter

Contents

Acknowledgments

I should like to express my gratitude to the many potters of Japan, especially fifth-generation potter Minoru Fukuda of Kasama and Tatsuzo Shimaoka of Mashiko; Pastor Tsugumichi Ohkawa and Zama Church; Emiko Kawada; Harbor Church; Chaplain Billy Dodson and family; Johnnie Mary Clary; the Miltons; Kay Varley; and the Semmlers.

Introduction

When we first begin a venture, we may not know the direction it will take. That was certainly true for me with the subject of pottery. When I began talking with potters in Japan about their craft, my aim was to tell them all about God. However, as the potters confided their simple respect for the clay and their hope for all it could become, they unknowingly drew for me, instead, a picture of the Master Potter, His patience, and His potential for mankind.

Those potters did not know God; they did not know that the Bible pictures God as the Potter and us as the clay. I longed to tell them all this in words they could comprehend. So I set out to write a pamphlet based on Isaiah 64:8: "O LORD, you are our Father. We are the clay, you are the potter; we are all the work of your hand." That pamphlet has become this book.

The chief role of the potter is to unbind what is bound. His singular aim is to release the clay to become all that it can become. The chief aim of this book is the same: to unbind a suffering humanity from fears that bind and from traditions and superstitions that weigh us down; to appeal to every person to be himself or herself in the sense of becoming all God intends them to be. Ultimately, however, this book is an intimate portrait of an intimate God, of how He has chosen us, tamed us, fashioned us, broken us, and resurrected us, even as the potter lifts the clay from the formless to the formed.

Each of us has unique work to do, unique contributions to make; there is no one who can take the place God has intended for us. In spite of all our faults and flaws, we are His masterpieces. We are masterpieces beyond comparison; we are designs that confound science and technology; we are the most complicated combination of molecules ever set in motion.

We are the worthy vessels of the Master Potter.

This is the word that came to Jeremiah from the LORD: "Go down to the potter's house, and there I will give you my message." So I went down to the potter's house, and I saw him working at the wheel. But the pot he was shaping from the clay was marred in his hands; so the potter formed it into another pot, shaping it as seemed best to him.

Then the word of the LORD came to me: "O house of Israel, can I not do with you as this potter does? . . . Like clay in the hand of the potter, so are you in my hand." Jeremiah 18:1–6

PART ONE

The Potter Frees the Clay

Choosing the Clay
Preparing the Clay
Resting the Clay

Even the most magnificent piece of pottery gets its start by first becoming particles of dust. . . . Finding the unknown and helping each to reach its potential—that is what the work of the potter is all about. . . . The preparation of clay for service is a long, slow process by which it gains its unusual strength and resilience.

Choosing the Clay

"And the LORD God formed man of the dust of the ground" (Genesis 2:7 KJV).

In an art exhibition in Tokyo one piece of pottery sits taller than all the others. Not because it is larger. In fact, it is a mere bowl. Rather, it has been set upon a pedestal to display its prize-winning qualities. Although the potter's name is written on a small card that stands beside the piece—along with a price tag of almost one thousand dollars, marked SOLD—the potter is not in evidence except through his creation.

This prize-winning bowl bears little resemblance to the lump of *clay* the potter first brought forth from a wild animal's deserted dugout on the mountain. The potter, looking for the possible, took the shapeless piece of earth and made it into this vessel of beauty and usefulness.

Clay has no apparent value of its own in a *raw* state; yet it can be made into objects of great value. The value is put there by the potter.

Analogy is unique to the human race. Our literature is written in symbols and our stories employ fantasy and metaphor. Even the Bible is a book filled with metaphors, and Jesus spoke in parables to help His followers understand His teachings.

One of the metaphors used throughout Scripture is that of the potter and the clay, implying that to explore the ways of the potter is to touch the edge of God's whereabouts; to understand the nature of the clay is to understand ourselves more fully.

Genesis 2:7 says that "the LORD God formed the man from the dust of the ground." Later, after Adam and Eve chose a lower lifestyle than God had intended, the destiny of their bodies became the place of their origin: "By the sweat of your brow you will eat your food until you return to the ground, since from it you were taken; for dust you are and to dust you will return" (Genesis 3:19).

"We are the clay," reckoned Isaiah. And scientists centuries later have noted that the chemical constituents of the human body do, in fact, compare with the chemistry of clay. "By his body

Adam was allied with the earth. Chemically the body of man differs not a particle from the earth out of which he was taken. The human body consists of about 85 percent water (hydrogen and oxygen), calcium, sodium, iron, nitrogen, phosphorus, arsenic, and a large number of rarer elements. This allies him closely to the inorganic creation."[1]

Both the Old Covenant and the New refer to men and women as clay vessels. Early on, the people themselves recognized the comparison. Job, the wealthiest man of his day, cried out, "Thou hast made me as the clay" (10:9 KJV). David, who became king of Israel, sang, "He brought me up also out of an horrible pit, out of the miry clay" (Psalm 40:2 KJV).

Adam, the first man, was "formed . . . of the dust of the ground" and God "breathed into his nostrils the breath of life; and man became a living soul" (Genesis 2:7 KJV). (Later on we shall see how some potters blow gently into the pot they are making at the *wheel* and what the warm breath inside the vessel does to bring out the life in the soft, pliable clay.) Interestingly, in the Hebrew language the name Adam implies "red" or "ruddy," and *adamah* means "earth."

In his second letter to the church at Corinth, the apostle Paul referred to the Christians as "earthen vessels" (KJV) or "jars of clay" (NIV) containing a treasure not seen by those who could not understand their faith. "But we have this treasure in earthen vessels, that the excellency of the power may be of God, and not of us" (2 Corinthians 4:7 KJV). Paul clearly defined that treasure as Jesus Christ living in us. This treasure inside these vessels is unique to the human race and not given to plants or animals. The very power and image of God Himself is contained in these human bodies of clay, these earthen vessels.

Eight centuries before Paul, however, Isaiah had already chosen the universal figure of the potter and the clay to represent God and humanity, His creation. It is a word picture that can be understood by people of any nationality, any educational level, any language.

What child has not rolled out a ball of clay and formed it into an image of his or her own choice? What person has not eaten or drunk from a dish or cup made of clay, or channeled water through reddish brown clay pipes, or walked on tiles baked in a potter's *kiln,* or planted flowers in a clay pot? Even as I type this, a simple clay mug sits at my fingertips, a thing of beauty and a vessel of service to hold my tea.

Somewhat later in the history of God's people, the prophet Jeremiah was told, "'Go down to the potter's house, and there I will give you my message'" (Jeremiah 18:2). Let us go there, too.

[2]

We stand at the potter's wheel and watch him with fascination.

He centers a lump of clay on the wheel, and with steady pressure his skillful hands pull the whirling mass into a cylinder. With apparent ease his thumbs form a hole in the cylinder, and the lump begins to take the shape of some sort of vessel. He cups the bottom of the cylinder with both hands and adds pressure in the middle of the pot with his thumbs, creating a squat, round base. While the shape continues to spin on the wheel, he wets his fingers. With gentle, artful movements his fingers tighten on the cylinder and mold a slender neck for the vase. In a matter of minutes the potter has formed a graceful vase from a formless lump of clay.

I recognize that women as well as men are potters, that there is nothing inherently masculine about pottery making. However, for the purpose of the analogy, I will use masculine pronouns to refer to the potter.

As we share these intimate moments with the master potter, we are strongly attracted to his craft. Part of the attraction is our need to create, having been created by the Creator Himself and bearing within us His image. The potter intrigues us with his adeptness at liberating the energy of the clay and his ability to free each piece of earth to individual beauty.

Perhaps a greater part of our attraction to his work, however, is the magnetic pull in our chemistry that strangely identifies with the clay itself. In the potter's hands the substance seems free enough to make mistakes, to be real, to hold desires that need satisfaction. We feel the touch as he pulls, stretches, and waits for the clay to become the best that is in it. And finally we hear him call it by name as it becomes the vessel he has created it to be in all its unique beauty, individual dignity, and special usefulness.

Through the potter's workmanship, the water, the rhythm of the wheel, and the fire, the clay is refined and changed through and through. When moist, clay is *plastic* and moldable. When dry, it is hard and brittle. When fired, its shape becomes permanent. And when a useful and pleasurable vessel eventually breaks, the broken fragments return to the earth where they persist as inconspicuous pebbles returning to the granite rock from which they came.

Of all the needs that potters have filled, drinking is perhaps the most basic. The first vessel was probably the cupped hand of a man or woman or child dipping up water from a stream or pond. Then the first potter made a little clay basin and called it a cup, a bowl, a jug, to serve this human need. If clay symbolizes humanity, then perhaps every human being should be like the cup, the bowl, the jug—both beautiful and useful. Do we see both traits in ourselves?

[3]

Clay is found in abundance around the world, a product of the decomposition and disintegration of those *feldspathic* and granite rocks that form three-fourths of the earth's surface. Some clays are pickaxed from the sides of mountains. Some are driven from their original habitat by a strong water hose that washes them from the mountain slope down to the bottom. Some were carried away from their original beds by streams and rivers in some far-off geological age and deposited where we find them today—in swamps where the rivers run slowly.

Clay is formed as a result of the physical or chemical *weathering* and decomposition of volcanic, feldspathic stone. Physical weathering of these stones takes place when water seeping into cracks in their surfaces expands on freezing and forces flakes and pieces of the mother stone to break away. (How gentle, yet how powerful, how pur- poseful is this water. No more appropriate element could have been used to characterize and symbolize the Holy Spirit.) Water, having no shape of its own, readily takes on the shape of the clay, gently moving into the hard spots, soaking and changing raw clay to usability. Gradually the earthlike pieces that have flaked off from the mother stone are reduced to still smaller particles by the actions of sunlight, wind, and rain. Oxygen and *carbon dioxide* in the air and soluble salts in rain water result in further decomposition and produce the fine particles that become clay. Thus, God uses the laws He has put into nature to effect His refining actions and reveal His higher plans.

The potter uses two kinds of clay. Defined in their simplest terms, they are *primary clays* and *secondary clays*.

Primary or residual clays are those found in the location of the mother rock.

Although these clays are often quite pure, they are difficult to work into a shape with any strength. They are not highly plastic, not easily pliable. Thus, in England the clay diggers are asked to leave the newly dug clay exposed to the weather for at least a year.

Much like the clay, we often need to be weathered for a while before we are ready for use. Moses was exposed to the weather—his life in Midian—before God could use him. Jacob spent twenty years under Laban's abuse before he was sufficiently weathered. His son Joseph, too, was weathered from the time he was seventeen until he was thirty.

Secondary clays, on the other hand, are those that have been transported away from the mother rock. As a result of the long process of being carried, they attain a fineness and uniformity of particle size that makes them much more pliable and fit for use, although they usually contain impurities because of their long exposure to the elements. These impurities, however, cause the rich grays, dark browns, blues, and blacks found in true secondary clays, for the colors are the result of organic impurities burning out during *firing*. And while these pliable and plastic transported clays make the best pots, they also have a higher percentage of *shrinkage* during firing.

In just such a way God takes our ugliness and turns it into beauty; He takes our weakness and converts it into strength. In the heat from our trials, our impurities are burned away, and beautiful patterns take their place. And as our weaknesses shrink away for the sake of His redemption, we are left firmer and stronger. We need not curse our past nor harbor guilt feelings for our shame of yesterday. We can arise with each new day and trust God to make our lives into something beautiful, something good. It is possible. It happens every day at the potter's house.

[4]

Jesus said, "Unless you change and become like little children, you will never enter the kingdom of heaven" (Matthew 18:3). Physical things look biggest when we are smallest. Likewise, spiritual littleness, or humbleness, or childlikeness, is the condition needed for perceiving great truth. Even the most magnificent piece of pottery began as particles of dust.

We watch at the potter's house in silence and remember times when we ourselves have felt small.

We remember times we fell, but like the clay, we could be lifted up to begin again and again. The potter's hand, like the hand of a loving God, is the hand of redemption. Furthermore, the potter always recognizes suitable clay when he finds it. He is able to distinguish it from mud or sand.

The small grandson of a famous potter in Mashiko, Japan, romping in the workshed one rainy afternoon, kicked the clay that sat waiting for the next *wedging*. Delighted by the impression of his shoe in the clay, the boy drew his other foot back ready to kick again when he was brought to a sudden stop as his father caught his foot from behind and firmly ordered him to stop. "See, you got mud on the clay," his father said as he pointed to the footprint.

The boy was only four, but he thought for a minute and asked, "Clay and mud, it's all the same, isn't it, daddy?"

The father scraped off the muddy footprint as he tried to explain the difference. Then he handed his son a generous handful of the gentle clay, along with a scoop of coarse mud, and sat down to watch his son fashion something. "You decide if they're the same," he challenged.

The potter knows the clay, and because he does, he searches it out and reaches into the right spot on the mountainside, though thorns may prick his hands in the searching. In spite of the thorns and bleeding scratches, he gathers the treasured clay.

26

God himself has gone out to find us, has bled for us, and has painstakingly taken us through many processes in preparation for making us beautiful and useful. Wherever we happen to be at this moment in the potter's process, however, we differ from the clay in one important way: He has planted a voice within us, and we can cry out to Him, "Wait for me. I'm coming. Don't give up on me." And in His infinite wisdom God may speak the same to us: "Wait for Me. Don't try to get ahead of Me. I will shape you in the form that is right for you."

From start to finish the Potter touches His clay and knows it for its perishability as well as its strength. Each piece becomes a work of His own hands. "You did not choose me, but I chose you," He says (John 15:16).

[5]

When I was in the fifth and sixth grades of elementary school, I used to play on the boys' baseball team. Because I was tall for my age—gangly was the word—they considered me a good hitter as well as a strong-arm thrower. I wanted to play first or third base, but I was afraid of the ball, so they put me out in left field. Although I had the power, I was never any good at controlling where the ball would go once I threw it, so I was really not much good to the team except when I was up to bat.

27

In this little country school we would choose teams every morning at recess. Two boys—Dick and Ronnie—were always the captains; they would flip a coin and call it, heads or tails, to see who would pick first. Then they would start choosing their teams.

Oh, it felt so good to hear my name called, to be chosen! The sooner my name got called, the harder I played. I remember hitting home runs for Ronnie one day, and the next day I was the first one chosen on Dick's side, as he had won the toss that day.

But one day I struck out. I don't recall whether the pitcher was unusually good that day or whether I was playing poorly, but I, the only girl batter, struck out. The guys did not like me any more, and the girls, who had been jealous of me, clapped their hands. The team did not like me because I cried, and I cried because they did not like me. But the taste of being chosen was so wonderful that I wished for it to happen all over again.

In that little East Texas country school we also had spelling bees at least once a week—or whenever we could talk the teacher into having one. It was a one-teacher classroom where three or four grades were together, and for the spelling bees everyone lined up on two sides of the room, and the race was on. Each side tried to outspell the other until the last person left standing brought his or her team to victory.

Nobody wanted John. He was an awful speller. Not only that, he had pimples. One day I had
the awesome responsibility of being one of the
choosers. I looked around the room at the faces of
all my friends. Everyone knew I would choose
Velma. She was the best speller in the room, and
whoever won the toss always chose Velma first
off. My mouth opened, and I called out my first
choice: "John!"

John popped up straight out of his seat. He
smiled so big you could not even see him; all you
could see was the happiness in his eyes. He stood
up from his desk, stuffed his pink shirt into his
orange pants, and strutted to the front of the
room—I'm sure he made it in two and a half
strides—the first time in his life he was not thirti-
eth among thirty. He stood beside me, his head
high. I believe he could have spelled hippopotamus.
He could have spelled Czechoslovakia. For the rest
of the day—in fact, for a whole week—I lost Velma as my best friend. I might have lost the spelling bee, too; I don't remember. But I have never
forgotten the smile on John's face or the taste of
being chosen.

Sometimes I get a taste of it again. I have
been John so many times I cannot count them.
And I have struck out just when expectations were
highest. But to be chosen—it still brings the same
excited glee I felt in that little schoolroom.

And to think that the Potter, almighty God
Himself, went out of His way to that country

place and found me. And He went to you and found you. Wherever I walk, in Japan, in Korea, in jungles of the South Pacific, in cities that dot the globe, I find the Potter has been there, too. I have come upon His handiwork many times, often in the least expected places. Quietly He searches, finds His clay, bends down to choose the formless, and rejoices over what it will become.

Listen for Him when He comes your way. "He will rejoice over you with singing" (Zephaniah 3:17).

Preparing the Clay

"Man looks at the outward appearance, but the LORD *looks at the heart" (1 Samuel 16:7).*

The eye of the potter is the eye of the artist; it sees beyond the shapeless lump of clay to the finished, refined vessel. Already as the potter searches in the hills and chooses his clay, he sees the completed pot, the vase, the tea cup; he already knows the water jug or the basin.

In this quality of the potter we see a picture of the omniscient God. Before we ever came into existence, before we were born, God saw us and chose us. Ephesians 1:4 tells us that "He chose us in him before the creation of the world to be holy and blameless in his sight." What a comfort in turbulent times to know that God not only knows us right now but knew us—one by one—before the world ever came into being.

The potter is the epitome of hope. He is a creator with vision for the future of the scoop of clay he holds in his hands. Whatever condition the clay is in, the potter will make it better. With the eye of hope he sees within the clay the potential for beauty, for strength, for use. It is the potter's dream to free that potential, to bring that beauty into existence.

Cheap, abundant, formless clay is deceptively simple material. Yet the potter has discovered two great truths about it: First, it improves with age; and second, it responds to blending, shaping, drying, firing, and smoothing.

This inherent ability to respond is also vital to men and women who aspire to reach a measure of their potential. Willingness to bend habits and respond to another way can make the difference between a stiff and awkward life and a flowing, healthy life. To be elastic and flexible; to respond to the message of the Bible; to expand our rigid schedules to include possibilities we meet along the way—all these can show us vistas we have never seen before.

Have you ever had a sudden urge to contact a certain person and later learned that the person was sick or in trouble at that very moment and needed you? Have you ever felt you ought to attend a

certain conference but did not know why, only to
have a once-in-a-lifetime experience while there?

Some people say, "Nothing exciting like that
ever happens to me." If that is true, then I say it
is because they were anticipating too far ahead and
neglected to respond to the still, small voice of
God at some earlier point. It is as we form a habit
of responding that we learn to discern the voice of
God from our own whims and thus get positioned
for the next step and the next. D'Israeli aptly said,
"The secret of success in life is to be ready when
the opportunity comes."

There is nothing like the pressure and scrutiny
of God to get us ready. Like the potter tending his
clay, God prepares each of us carefully, for the
possibilities are so vast. Our chances are limited
only by our apathy. By our responses, we move
on and ever onward.

Because the potter lives in the hope that from
a shapeless lump of clay will emerge a vessel of
worth, he is willing to endure the slow, tedious
process of preparing the clay for its moment on
the wheel.

[2]

Preparation requires patience. The potter has
learned through years of experience that the preparation of the clay must not be rushed. In the work
of the Mashiko potter in Japan, the clays of various colors are sorted and pounded by hand. The

strata in the earth contain different types of clay, each of different texture and color. Like human personalities, some clays are coarse, some fine; some are gray, some yellow or brown, which means they contain oxides that will mellow the final color during firing. Some potters mix the types; some use each clay individually. Whichever method is preferred, the preparation of clay for service is a long, slow process by which it gains its unusual strength and resilience.

After the clays are pounded into fine particles, they are spread out in fist-sized piles to dry. Then they are carried to tanks dug deep in the ground where they are mixed with water. Sand sinks to the bottom, the water rises, and impurities are removed as the fine liquid *slip* is screened very wet between two settling tanks. The potter, his wife, and helpers stir this pure clay mixture with a long wooden oar; they ladle and sieve it back and forth for several days before ladling it into shallow settling troughs made of hard clay. The clay cannot be hurried.

After a few days of moisture evaporation, the potter scoops the clay *slurry* from these troughs into *bisque* pots for further drying to the plastic, workable state. It is hard work. It is demanding work. It is a tedious and persistent process to bring the clay from its mountainside habitat or rocky field to this smooth and workable state. Though retaining its original chemistry, by this point the clay has given up its own identity.

34

We, like the clay, respond to the Master Potter as He patiently prepares us for use. We, too, give up our own identity, entrusting ourselves fully to the Potter's hand as we are sorted, broken down, screened, mixed—prepared for usefulness. Sometimes we resist this preparation, wanting to avoid the pain that we fear the process may inflict on us. Or we become impatient with the time the Potter takes to prepare us. And yet if He rushed the process, the results could be disastrous.

Shinsaku Hamada, the son of one of Japan's leading potters, the late Shoji Hamada, participated in a potters' workshop in California in 1963. Using the commercially mixed American clay from machines, Hamada thought he could build a bigger slab rectangular pot than he usually did at his home shop in Mashiko, Japan. He worked with the fine skills he had learned from his father and accumulated from his own experiences, and his California pots looked good. But one by one they all cracked. Those big pots that looked so beautiful broke as they dried.

The cause of the cracking was the inferior plasticity of American clay—inferior because of the Americans' lack of understanding about the importance of time spent in preparation. "Americans don't comprehend clay, the long stages of preparation necessary to make raw clay plastic and strong so that it won't crack in drying or firing," Shinsaku Hamada concluded. "Clay must be processed for days, and wedged by hand a long time. Americans and English just do not use enough 'arm.' Working the clay over and over by hand can't be duplicated by machine."[2]

The hand-wedging (*kneading*) at Mashiko may take two hours, depending on the consistency required for the various shapes of pots to be made.

Japanese folk pottery, as well as that of the American Indians, involves a long, patient process by hand. The potters take care in finding the clay in the first place, then in mixing it and aging it. "Think of all the thin pot shapes you have seen made by the American Indians for centuries," said Hamada. "They had to have chosen and prepared the clay very carefully to be able to make those shapes."[3]

Slow changes help bring the clay to maturity. Each step builds upon the other and promotes a progressive refinement. Indeed, without this training, clay would be impotent.

If the changes are too abrupt, the clay may not have the staying power to last. So, too, in our human journey through life there are times when it is necessary to move slowly and maintain a staying power, a depth of commitment to our beliefs.

In school I used to wonder why a three-to-five-page theme was required in English class every week without fail. A one-page paper would not only have been faster for the teacher to read, but the shorter one would also reveal as much of the student's grammatical competence as the longer one. I wondered why they assigned fifty algebra problems instead of ten. Only later did I realize that this system of education had developed a quality in me that might otherwise have remained dormant; over and above any skill and knowledge that might have been a by-product, I had been infused with a powerful dose of perseverance. "Stick-to-itiveness" was the word Americans coined for that quality of character that enables a person to see something through to the very end, a sustaining power over the long haul.

The skillful potter knows that time and care produce the best results. A potter can pull up the clay on the wheel and form a perfect pot in minutes. It takes him no time at all to turn out five or six pots from a single lump of clay—that is, only if the clay has been thoroughly prepared and properly conditioned.

Some potters age their clay as long as five years after removing certain impurities from the raw material. To any of us who lack the expertise to appreciate the exacting work of time on chemistry, this wait may seem to be a waste of time. But the potter knows that his willingness to wait may mean the difference between a mediocre vessel and one of great worth.

Similarly, God's wisdom often includes a slow process of preparation and long periods of waiting. Abraham was seventy-five years old when God first announced that He would make him the father of many nations; childless Abraham was to become the father of innumerable descendants. Yet Abraham and Sarah waited twenty-five years more before they had Isaac, their son of promise.

God's preparation of the apostle Paul also involved a long waiting period. After Paul's dramatic conversion, he was eager to begin preaching the gospel, but God had other plans. He sent Paul into the Arabian desert, where he spent three years; only after these years of quiet instruction was Paul ready to begin his active and sometimes stormy ministry.

We do not always understand God's purposes in our lives. We do not always understand the periods of waiting that He gives to us. But seeing ourselves as clay, we can be confident that our lives are in process and that we are in the hands of a wise and knowing Master Potter. He is not careless. He wants the best for us. He knows what He is doing with each of us and knows what kind of preparation we need. He takes great care with us, His earthen vessels. But He waits for a certain response from us; for in the measure that we respond to His leading, He continues working His higher plans for us.

[3]

Before the clay is ready to be used on the wheel, the potter often adds substances to it, wedging or kneading to work in the additives.

For the sake of forming, clay has to be plastic; but if it is too plastic, it becomes extremely difficult to handle. In such instances, nonplastic substances are added to the clay to keep plasticity at the desired level, to control firmness, and to increase the *porosity,* which helps the clay dry without shrinking or cracking. Today few clays are used for pottery work without some adjustment to increase their good properties and reduce their faults.

Silica is one of the additives that a potter kneads into the clay. Silica promotes the fusing of the other materials while giving added strength and stability to the fired *ware.*

In addition to silica, *grog* is often added to native clay. Grog is made simply from pulverized *refractory* bricks or previously fired pottery; the fineness of the resulting powder depends on the use to which it will be put. In general, all grogs increase porosity, speed drying, minimize shrinkage, prevent cracking and *warping* during firing, and make the clay stiffer and easier to *throw* or mold into large forms.

"Is there any use for those old pots behind the kiln?" I asked one afternoon at a potter's place in the village. "Those plates that stuck to each other in the firing, and the cups that sit squatty with broken handles?" That was when I learned the value of grog. I had figured that once a pot or vessel had hardened in its deformity, it was beyond use—to be discarded. But actually the new clay is made stronger by mixing in some of the pulverized form of the clay that has already gone through the fire.

Those pieces forfeit their own shape, their own identity, their own purpose for which they had been created, so that a new and stronger vessel may come into being. And only in the perfect blending of the two can the one be prevented from cracking and warping.

Jesus taught a parallel idea: "I tell you the truth, unless a kernel of wheat falls to the ground and dies, it remains only a single seed. But if it dies, it produces many seeds" (John 12:24).

Clay that is too soft may bend with the least resistance; clay that is too wet may warp and come out lopsided. Only clay that has received a proper blending, mixed by the master's hand, can be stretched into shape and remain strong.

Be it a pot of clay, a church composed of various age groups, or a successful business firm spreading into many branches, what organized body does not exemplify the overlay of old and new? The strength lies in the blending of the old and the new. The young person is wise who absorbs strengthening from the older person who has experienced the adversities of life. The older person is wise who listens to the discoveries of the young.

Along with silica and grog, various fusing materials such as *feldspar,* felsite, or semi-weathered granite are often added to the clay to promote fusion and coherence in the vessel. Felsite, which is used in the preparation of both clay and *glazes,* melts and mixes with the particles of the clay, binding them together. This binding makes the clay water–resistant and makes the receptacle not only pleasant to look at but also capable of doing the work for which it was made.

Just as the potter adds silica or grog or felsite to the clay to make it strong, so God adds to our lives those experiences and qualities that will make us strong and productive. In his epistles Peter recognized that we need spiritual additives:

> Make every effort to add to your faith goodness; and to goodness, knowledge; and to knowledge, self-control; and to self-control, perseverance; and to perseverance, godliness; and to godliness, brotherly kindness; and to brotherly kindness, love. For if you possess these qualities in increasing measure, they will keep you from being ineffective and unproductive in your knowledge of our Lord Jesus Christ (2 Peter 1:5–8).

Like the felsite, which when it reaches the melting point is able to bind together all components of the clay to make the vessel strong against leaks or abuse, love is a binding force which knits together all the disparate elements to make a family or body indomitable against trials, betrayal, or any of the storms of life.

[4]

Not only is it necessary to add materials to certain clays, but it is imperative that all clay be free from dangerous impurities. Lime disqualifies a clay for kiln work. Lime or bits of limestone cannot be tolerated in a clay, for when lime is fired, it is altered from calcium carbonate to calcium oxide. Calcium oxide is an unstable oxide in the atmosphere because it hydrates, or takes on water. This hydration, which will go on slowly even in a small lump of limestone buried in a fired clay object, causes the lime to swell. The swelling exerts an irresistible pressure against the fired clay that surrounds the bit of lime and the piece will break, or a flake of clay will break off, revealing the troublesome impurity. This breaking off or *flaking* will occur within a few days or months after firing, depending on how porous the clay body is and on the humidity to which it is exposed.[4]

Any stone, no matter how tiny to the touch of the finger, must be removed from the clay before the clay can be worked into a potter's *bung,* ready for further wedging and forming on the wheel. That minute but stubborn impediment can wreck the finest of pots if left until the firing stage. A pretty stone may manage to bury itself under the surface and be covered over by other beautiful traits in the clay vessel—until the final testing. In the firing, the tiniest stone manifests itself. It punches a hole in the pot and rejects the glaze on that spot. If it happens on the lip of a vase, the value of the vase is reduced to almost nothing. If it works through the body of a water pot or a pitcher, it makes the vessel useless, fit only for the discard heap or, at best, a dusty shelf somewhere.

Like the potter, God is ever at work, kneading

our lives to work out the hardened flaws in our characters. Through the Holy Spirit, He shows us the sin and impurities in our lives, and through His Son Jesus, He cleanses us and purifies us, making us usable. Just as the potter is patient and persistent in making sure that each speck of lime or tiny stone has been removed from the clay, God is patient and persistent in rooting out of our lives any flaws and sins that would mar us and make us unfit later on.

We are often painfully aware of those areas in our character that have to be worked out of us like pesky stones that ruin the clay—our stubborn refusal to admit personal error, our unwillingness to obey the requests of those in authority, our busybodyness, and our sneaky deeds.

In the case of clay, if lime cannot be removed, the clay is discarded and passed over for other clay that can be used.

If we have rebellious and careless tendencies in our character that will damage the development of our work, the Lord, like the knowing potter, will be our judge. The Bible says that "He will bring to light what is hidden in darkness and will expose the motives of men's hearts" (1 Corinthians 4:5).

Let us pray not for an easy life but for a purifying journey. Let us pray not for God's permission to do what we want to do but for His persistence to do what He wants to do.

[5]

Today, the casual visitor to a potter's place may seldom, if ever, see people treading the clay with their feet, but I have seen it on occasion in Japan. It seemed that the potters were reducing the clay to paste, walking upon the mound of clay until it oozed between their bare toes. Their purpose was to bring it to the right consistency; it was not done gently, but with determination to conquer and bring the clay to submission. In Asia, the act of using the foot rather than the hand seems to signify a sort of judgment. In the cultures of that part of the world, it is improper to move a cushion with the foot; it is improper to shove a door closed or open with the foot. If the hands are full, one must put the things down and open or close the door with the hand. The foot is reserved for a type of judgment, similar perhaps to the treading of grapes in Revelation.

It was winter when I observed the treading of the clay, and the clay was stiff and unyielding until trodden under foot. Then, and only then, was it able to take shape from the touch of the master's hand. Only clay that is flexible and adaptable ever achieves its true identity.

God, too, sometimes treads in the winter of our lives bringing us to a point of pliability and yieldedness. We need not see God's discipline of us as negative.

"My son, do not make light of the Lord's discipline, and do not lose heart when he rebukes you, because the Lord disciplines those he loves, and he punishes everyone he accepts as a son."

Endure hardship as discipline; God is treating you as sons. For what son is not disciplined by his father? If you are not disciplined (and everyone undergoes discipline), then you are illegitimate children and not true sons. Moreover, we have all had human fathers who disciplined us and we respected them for it. How much more should we submit to the Father of our spirits and live! Our fathers disciplined us for a little while as they thought best; but God disciplines us for our good, that we may share in his holiness. No discipline seems pleasant at the time, but painful. Later on, however, it produces a harvest of righteousness and peace for those who have been trained by it.

Therefore, strengthen your feeble arms and weak knees (Hebrews 12:5–12).

Perhaps God was "treading" on Jacob when He wrestled with him at Peniel. God forced him down so that Jacob, unable to move, had to surrender. Jacob emerged from the encounter with a limp that would be an ever-present reminder that God had touched his life—that God was in control. But through this experience Jacob was also given a new name and a new identity—Israel, the apple of God's eye.

The master potter is not always gentle, but he is ever patient, persistent, and full of hope. He waits a long time for his clay to go through washings, settlings, dryings, more washings, evaporations, mixings, treadings, resting, aging. Then, when the textured clay is just right for shaping, he gives the inner life of the clay a chance to come out.

When the clay is the softness of the human ear lobe, the potters say, it is right for forming. It is then that the potter kneads his clay with his hands and covers it with plastic or wet cloth, seals it tightly so that it will not dry out, and leaves it to rest for a week to ten days.

> O Lord, teach me how to hope. Like the clay, bend me, I pray; and help me to yield to Your wish. Touch me today, and cause me to rise up tomorrow.

46

Resting the Clay

"He makes me lie down" (Psalm 23:2).

Rest for the clay is extremely important. During the rest period the air escapes from the clay and it forms a more even texture. Rest increases the plasticity of the clay so that it will not crack during the forming of the pot.

No potter neglects the rest period for his clay, for he knows the clay's potential is diminished if it does not rest. No potter hurries his clay through this step, for he knows that clay that is sufficiently rested makes the best pottery.

For a majority of people, rest is a result of tiredness; it is something that follows exhaustion after the completion of something big. On the contrary, rest is the prerequisite for events to come. It is not the end; it is the beginning. It is not the aftermath; it is the preliminary. It is not a result but a cause.

It was the sixth day on which Adam and Eve were created, and they were commanded to rest on the next day, the day God rested, the seventh day. Yet Adam and Eve had had no part in the great creation. Their rest day was actually their first day. They were not commanded to rest *after* they had done any labor but *before*.

When I go to bed at night, I often take my leave of others who are still up by announcing that I am going to my room to make preparations for tomorrow. Those who know me know that means I am going upstairs to go to sleep. Some go to bed because they are tired, worn out, sleepy. I like to think that I go to bed so that the next day will be mine to use to its fullest and at my best. I can hardly wait for the next morning. But a night of rest is my preparation time, and I have found no substitute for it. If I want my mind as well as my eyes to be sharp the next day, I have to turn in early. Admittedly, it is largely because of my eyes that I am forced to stop in the evenings, but I am thankful for this warning signal from my body so that by even this forced way of resting, I can be prepared for the next morning.

Just as the potter knows that the texture of the clay will become even only after the clay has

48

rested, God requires the "evening" effect of rest for our existence and our function.

One of the blights of our time is the fast pace, the speed with which we live. Yet even a cursory look at the design of all living things, whether animals or plants, shows that their optimum development and productivity are in direct relationship to their periods of rest. What might appear to be inactivity may be a time of rebuilding worn-out cells, reconditioning tired tissues, or producing nutrients. For humans, rest is necessary for preparation and procreation of the spiritual, mental, emotional, and physical life.

God knows the importance of rest for His creation. Not only did He give us a model to follow by resting on the seventh day of His creation, but He also set down laws and guidelines in the Old Testament that commanded His people—indeed, all of creation—to rest.

> "Six days do your work, but on the seventh day do not work, so that your ox and your donkey may rest and the slave born in your household, and the alien as well, may be refreshed" (Exodus 23:12).

> "Six days you shall labor, but on the seventh day you shall rest; even during the plowing season and harvest you must rest" (Exodus 34:21).

So strong were the commands, that the penalty for non-rest was death.

"For six days, work is to be done, but the seventh day shall be your holy day, a Sabbath of rest to the LORD. Whosoever does any work on it must be put to death" (Exodus 35:2).

By disobeying the call to rest, people in today's society are subjecting themselves to the death penalty proclaimed in Exodus. Instead of using the Sabbath as a day of rest as God intended, people use the Sabbath as a day to catch up on their work or to squeeze in one more activity. It is no wonder that these same people find their lives overextended and overstimulated. It is no wonder that those who do not rest every seventh day find themselves with high blood pressure or headaches or heart conditions.

God knows that our lives need the balance of rest and work, quietness and activity. So He explicitly gave us a time to work and a time to rest.

In the Old Testament the Levitical laws even included a rest for the land every seventh year and every fiftieth year—known to the Jews as the year of Jubilee, when they lived day to day rather than by harvesting and saving.

"For six years sow your fields, and for six years prune your vineyards and gather their crops. But in the seventh year the land is to have a sabbath of rest, a sabbath to the LORD. Do not sow your fields or prune your vineyards. Do not reap what grows of itself or harvest the grapes of your untended vines. *The land is to have a year of rest.* Whatever the land yields during the sabbath year will be food for you—for yourself, your manservant and maidservant, and the hired worker and temporary resident who live among you, as well as for your livestock and the wild animals in your land. Whatever the land produces may be eaten" (Leviticus 25:3–7, italics mine).

By telling them to rest their land, the God of the universe offered people not only the chance to trust Him but also the chance to improve their lot; He said, "I will send you such a blessing in the sixth year that the land will yield enough for three years" (Leviticus 25:21).

In countries where farmers ignore the seventh year of rest for their land, it is an interesting phenomenon of agriculture that their vegetables are weaker in vitamin and mineral content than those vegetables that are grown on rested land. When farmers ignore the need of the soil to rest from producing the same crop or the same family of plants year after year, bugs seem to take over the plants, and the soil itself is depleted of certain nutrients and minerals necessary for its life. Soil that is overworked may be as pitiful as the human that is overworked. Death is the result.

God's creation needs rest. Even the construction engineer wisely allows rest time for the ground to settle the foundation of any building. Look at a gigantic skyscraper or any spreading piece of architecture in a modern metropolis, and know that the ground beneath it was dug and mixed and scraped and poured—and then left to rest before building was continued. Rest is a stabilizer that gives balance to life.

It is often in the resting that the remainder of life takes on meaning. Rests are deliberately written into music; they are a part of every great symphony. Without rests there is no music, only noise.

The most powerful speeches and the most dramatic moments, the best news commentaries and the most effective readings are achieved not so much by eloquence as by the mastery of pauses.

It is the empty spaces on a page, the rests between letters, that give form and meaning, that give words their identity. Without rest there can be only chaos.

[2]

Inexperienced potters often try to ignore the importance of resting the clay. In an attempt to move more quickly to the actual forming of the pot on the wheel, the potter lacking expertise and patience will skip the resting period only to find that the clay will crack while he is trying to form the pot. Clay that is not evenly textured will not hold up on the wheel; it will crack under the strain.

How similar we are to the potter's clay. When our bodies are not given the proper rest—both on a daily and a weekly basis—they start to break down. Without the proper balance of rest and activity, our lives begin to show cracks. When we constantly ignore the importance of rest and quietness, when we push ourselves to do more, to see more, to experience more, to be more, we can soon reach a breaking point.

We need only read our newspapers and journals to know that the pressures faced by business executives, by harried parents at home with young children, and by university students often lead to heart disorders, ulcers, migraine headaches—any number of physical or mental disorders. Doctors warn against the dangers of stress from overly committed schedules or stress brought on by ceaseless activity; they tell us to rest. Our bodies need time to even out, to stabilize, to balance out, or we, like the potter's clay, will crack.

A doctor's first advice to heart patients is "Slow down. Rest." For diseases of the liver, the sophisticated world of modern medicine admits no cure; but doctors do advise nutritional food, chewed slowly, and rest—especially after eating, just as the sheep are made to do in the Twenty-third Psalm. Pathologists admit that medication, while easing the symptoms, can invoke liver damage, and that rest is the only successful recommendation.

Rest and peace of mind are mandatory for the human body, yet many seem to fear stillness, silence, solitariness. Extended pauses in conversation are often considered painful lapses to be filled as quickly as possible. We fear the penetrating quality of silence. We cannot stand to be alone. We turn on the TV just for noise in the room, even if we are not watching it. To sit still and think our own thoughts seems unheard of or something to be avoided at all cost—and the cost is high.

I have asked Japanese university students why they read comic books and true-confession magazines. Is it because the stories are interesting? More than half of them say the stories are dull, but it is a way to kill time. They must fill the space.

Others use television to relax. To escape from the headaches or the boredom of their real world, they transfer themselves from their personal situation and whereabouts to an adventure world that is no less complex than their own and that, if they were really there, would be equally burdensome as their own. Such escapist fare, they say, is restful.

There is a time to do and a time to rest from doing. There is a time to take in and a time to give out. Today there are fewer and fewer of those who give out—writers, artists, composers, inventors. Creativity requires space; it requires time to be silent, time to be alone. Are we losing the art of stillness, of thought and meditation, the art of resting?

A few people may look forward to times of rest with eager anticipation, but most push themselves to their uttermost limits before giving in to a total weariness or exhaustion that demands they rest. Even toddlers fight away sleep when they are fatigued, afraid they might miss something. For some reason, perhaps the pace of modern living, we equate rest with laziness, yet this should not be. Rest is essential to our effectiveness; rest is a positive and productive aspect of living.

We constantly tell others how busy we are, making it sound pretty clear that there is little if any empty space inside us or around us for their presence. Yet often the busiest people are also the loneliest people in the world. When we leave no empty spaces for other people to enter our lives, we hurt them and ourselves.

When God said, "Be still, and know that I am God" (Psalm 46:10), did He foresee that we would become dependent on the noises and movements about us? Did He know that we would wake up to a blaring alarm clock, rush around to get dressed, and gobble our breakfast to the frantic rhythm of television or radio? With pressures on every side to run faster, to go further, and to do more, are we in danger of neglecting one of God's vital commands? If so, are we paying the price for our failure to be still and to listen to our Father's voice?

Even in our worship we need to learn the value of stillness and, yes, of rest. Can we more fully and effectively worship God during a period of silence at the right moment than in the hustle of standing for this hymn and sitting for that hymn and rushing through to the announcements of all the next week's agenda? Many churchgoers have quit going not because they quit believing but because they could not stand the fast pace of modern worship and the hasty greetings of their friends who are always off to the next committee meeting. I suspect that much of the weight of busyness we carry is a cross we have built ourselves. No matter how large and sophisticated the church, or how small, there must be a time to rest as well as a time to work. For without rest, the inner growth of the church will be stunted and the body will malfunction.

Can we learn a lesson from the potter and the clay? To give meaning to activity, to keep our lives in balance, to prevent our bodies and minds from cracking, we have to rest. In the quiet times we will find wholeness, joy, and creative inspiration.

[3]

Not only does the potter rest the clay to ward off the risk of cracking but he also rests the clay so that it can be used for a higher purpose. As the clay rests for several days, the water gently permeates the particles of the clay, improving the plasticity of the mass. The potter finds that at the end of the rest, the clay is more pliable and ready to be shaped.

We see ourselves in the metaphor. When we quiet our lives long enough to rest and be still before God, then He is able to shape and direct us.

It is not the rushed, loud, and ostentatious

prayers that call down the presence of God; rather, it is in quiet moments alone with Him that people gain inner peace and hear His voice. During that time of rest, the Great Physician is able to work in a way He could not while the person's mind and body were distracted by unrestful cares and activities. I have observed people resting in the Spirit for three hours at a time, others for two or three minutes. Strange, but during that time their minds could flash back to some disturbing episode that had happened to them years before, and Jesus could walk into that scene and make all things right; they had rest from it then and there.

Recurring headaches as well as painful arthritis can be the result of a build-up of unforgiveness, and release from these sufferings can come when the spiritual matter is dealt with and there is rest from it. When there is rest from fear, guilt, pent-up anger, stinginess, resentment, and pride, many physical diseases are also cleared up, including hypertension, stomach ulcers, indigestion, schizophrenia, pimples, asthma, heartburn, to name a few.

"Come to me," invited Jesus, "all you who are weary and burdened, and *I will give you rest*" (Matthew 11:28, italics mine). Where the human method is unforgiveness and grudges (resulting in crippling and pain), Jesus' method is forgiveness and absolving of one's anger by bedtime (resulting in freedom and health). "Do not let the sun go down while you are still angry" (Ephesians 4:26).

Because our emotions directly affect our physical health, the Bible calls us to quiet our minds and rid ourselves of feelings that damage us. As up to date as the latest medical journals, the Bible notes that "Resentment kills a fool, and envy slays the simple" (Job 5:2). When we dare to follow Jesus, He will give us rest from these agonizing and murderous emotions.

When good people do not take time to rest, to dream, to create, then people of worthless aims may take over. Read the life stories of the despots of history, and in each one you will find a person who recognized the power and value of quiet times to think, to plan, to rest. Chairman Mao Tse-tung in his youth led the peasant revolution in China, commanding his band of followers from place to place; but wherever they camped, the young leader first of all saw that he had some sort of desk or private chamber set apart from the busy routines of his men. Oh, he was out there with them, not miles away in a plush office; but even out in the field, he took hours every day to sit in a quiet place and think. That's all. A quiet place to still his mind. And he ruled a quarter of the world's population for a quarter of a century, and in very real ways he continues to wield power from his grave. Hitler, Stalin, Napoleon—even as far back as Alexander the Great—all leaders who have left a mark on history were those who rested themselves from the routines of life and the constant presence of others.

Dreams come in the night while we sleep.

Creative thinking comes in the hours of quiet meditation—when we stop everything else and are able to see life goals come clearly into focus. Some people never slow down long enough to see clearly, to think, to plan, or to achieve their full potential.

The light bulb, the telephone, the violin, the piano, all are results of ideas conceived in the minds of people who were quiet and still; they were born of patient and tedious trial and error. Thomas Edison, George Washington Carver, Madame Curie, Alexander Graham Bell, and an endless list of men and women who have contributed things of great worth to the world were people who dared to be still and know.

George Washington Carver, the famous American scientist, helped farmers improve their land by *resting* it from producing the same crops year in and year out. "Rotate your crops," he told farmers. "Give the soil a chance to breathe, substitute sweet potatoes or peanuts for the cotton, which is draining the land of its richness." As a child growing up on a southern plantation, George had rambled alone in the woods, humming and singing and picking all kinds of herbs. In the later years of his life, after fame had become an annoying invasion of his privacy, he was approached one day by a news reporter who asked him for his philosophy of life. Dr. Carver gave this answer: "I go into the woods and there I gather specimens and study the great lessons that Nature is eager to teach us.

Alone in the woods each morning I best hear and understand God's plan for me."5

The story is told that on one of his quiet, solitary walks in the woods Carver stopped and prayed, "Lord, what is the universe really made for?"

From somewhere within, he seemed to hear an answer. "That's too big a subject for you, my son. Ask Me about something smaller."

A few minutes later, he asked, "Lord, what was man made for?"

"Little man, you still want to know too much. Cut down the extent of your request and improve the intent."

Finally George stooped to the ground and prayed, "Lord, I want to know all about the lowly peanut. Please tell me about this little peanut."

Carver related later: "The Great Creator replied to me that my mind was too small to know *all* about the peanut, but He said He would give me a handful of peanuts. And He reminded me that He had said, 'I give you every seed-bearing plant on the face of the whole earth and every tree that has fruit with seed in it. They will be yours for food. And to all the beasts of the earth and all the birds of the air and all the creatures that move on the ground—everything that has the breath of life in it—I give every green plant for food. And it was so' (Genesis 1:29–30)."

And George Carver believed that it was so. He took his handful of peanuts into the laboratory and took them apart as he believed God had instructed him to do, separating the water, fats, oils, gums, resins, sugars, starches, amino acids, pectose, and pentosan. "I looked at God again and He looked at me," said Carver, "and I asked again, 'Why did you make the peanut?'"

"The Creator said, 'I have given you three laws: namely, compatibility, temperature, and pressure. All you have to do is take these constituents and put them together, observing these laws, and I will show you why I made the peanut.'"[6]

When the farmers became distraught with acres and acres of peanuts without a market, the aging Dr. Carver appeared before the House Ways and Means Committee in Washington, D.C., where he was given ten minutes to appeal for help on behalf of the farmers. Almost two hours later, after he had displayed more than 145 useful products made from peanuts, and a hundred more from sweet potatoes, every Congressman sat awed by the staggering variety of goods that could come from the lowly peanut—flour, coffee, shampoo, ink, polishes, face cream, pickles, cheese, and other unimaginable things. Because of a restful and quiet walk alone in the woods, his belief in God, and meditative experiments and daring in the laboratory, George Washington Carver turned the tables so that the problem in 1921 was no longer to find a market, but to supply enough peanuts.

There is power in being still. In the spiritual kingdom, in the world of science and music, literature or medicine, to be still, to rest, is part of the process. Great composers sat and dreamed, and in their stillness music floated up to them. Great works of literature were written by those whose minds grew sensitive to nature in quiet stillness, by those who learned to shut out the world to communicate with the depths of the human heart.

It is in the stillness that we hear the voice of God. Through times in which we are forced to rest, God shapes us and uses us.

George Frederic Handel went through a prolific period in his career; then he hit a slump. For months he was unable to compose anything, not even his thoughts. Becoming too busy with the routines that his job and society demanded of him, Handel's life was so hectic for a while that he was at times unable to finish a piece until two weeks before its opening.

Although a relentless artistic urge drove him onward, it has been said that if he had died at the end of his first fifty-five years of life, no one would recall his name today. It seemed that for every success he had a comparable failure. Growing more and more frustrated, Handel tried harder to create some new acceptable piece of music. Nothing came. In his frustration he could produce nothing except piles and piles of paper wadded up and tossed into the trash. In desperation, he gave up, his body too exhausted to try any more.

Handel withdrew into himself, and neither his best friends nor his closest colleagues saw him for almost a year. He was physically worn out, mentally drained, and spiritually barren.

For eleven months he rested from composing. Then one night as he lay stretched out across his bed, almost sleeping, he began to hear long and beautiful strains of music floating up to his ears; he lay still and listened. Where was it coming from? What was it? It sounded new to his ears, fresh and magnificent. He sat up and started to write what he "heard," and he could hardly write fast enough; the music kept flowing and flowing, bending and moving and dipping back to pick up a phrase in another key.

For twenty-four days Handel wrote. From Saturday, August 22, 1741, to Monday, September 14, 1741, he did not leave his house at Upper Brook Street.[7] Emerging from his long rest and working almost around the clock, he wrote page after page. At times when supper was brought to him, he had not yet touched his lunch.

Seven months later that music was presented for the first time and was so well received in Dublin that it was later performed in London in 1743. When the chorus began the mighty "Hallelujah," the audience, which included King George II, was so stirred that they rose from their seats and remained standing throughout the grand finale.[8] And it was this composition, the *Messiah,* that became Handel's masterpiece and continues to be performed all over the world today.

The *Messiah* was composed because George

Frederic Handel had rested from composing. To be still, to be at rest, is not taking time away from the production process. Rather, it is part of the process. It is so necessary that it cannot be left out.

The Potter in His infinite wisdom rests His clay—in hopes for its achievement tomorrow.

Father, help me rest myself from yesterday, for the promise of tomorrow that You can see in me.

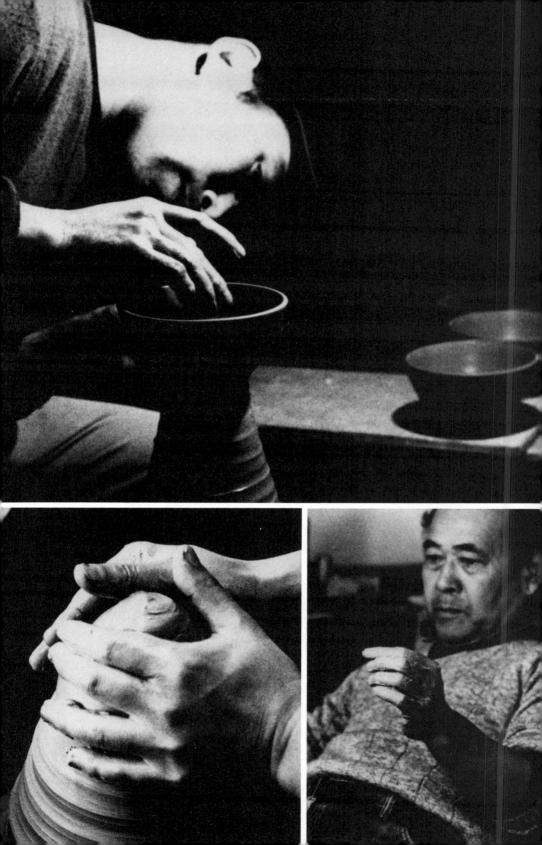

PART TWO

The Potter Names the Clay

Deciding the Vessel
Forming the Vessel

In their simple respect for the clay and their hope for all that it can become, the potters of Japan taught me of the patience of God. . . . Slow changes help bring the clay to maturity. . . . Although it takes a lot of time, each step builds upon the other and promotes a progressive refinement. . . . Without this training, the clay would be impotent. . . . The potter imposes certain conditions on his clay not to constrict it but to support it, not to enfeeble it but to empower it.

Deciding the Vessel

"Thine eyes did see my substance, yet being unperfect; and in thy book all my members were written, which in continuance were fashioned, when as yet there was none of them" (Psalm 139:16 KJV).

No vase or bowl or cup just happens. All vessels have their genesis in the potter's mind. Each vessel is a response to a clear-cut decision that the potter makes before ever setting the wheel in motion.

I have observed hundreds of skilled potters working at the wheel, and not once have I seen a potter change his mind in the middle of forming a vessel (for example, deciding to make a slender pitcher and then turning it into a bowl). Even though the clay may have a natural tendency to spread another way and stubbornly resist being raised, the knowing potter cups his strong hands around the clay and with patience and persistence has his will. Not unlike parents who know best for their children, the potter starts over as many times as necessary. His determination is not mixed with anger; his touch is loving.

As the potter works in silence, matching the image in his mind to the rhythm of the wheel, a warm rapport develops between the master and the mass of earth swirling between his hands. As we watch, we see the vessel as a three-dimensional object having height, breadth, and depth. But the potter sees it in four dimensions: height, breadth, depth, and unity; for he can see its unity with the image that is in his mind. Like the split-image focusing device of a camera, the image and the reality come together as one. The master potter is able to enjoy his creation in a closer dimension than the rest of us who can only see the outside.

In the beginning the potter conceives a clear image in his mind of the shape, the purpose, and the name of the vessel he has chosen to form at that moment on the wheel. In that little handful of earth he sees and names . . . a pitcher . . . a cup . . . a vase. Then he focuses all of his skill to masterfully call the vessel into being. It is his recognition that gives the clay worth.

David, the Old Testament king of Israel, recognized that God was like the potter. In one of his psalms, David expresses the wonderful mystery of the recognition of the Potter: before God called him into being, He knew him—knew his name, and knew the purpose for which he was to exist.

> O Lord, you have searched me and you know me. You know when I sit and when I rise; you perceive my thoughts from afar. You discern my going out and my lying down; you are familiar with all my ways. . . . You hem me in, behind and before; you have laid your hand upon me. . . . For you created my inmost being; you knit me together in my mother's womb. . . . My frame was not hidden from you when I was made in the secret place. When I was woven together in the depths of the earth, your eyes saw my unformed body (Psalm 139:1–3, 5, 13, 15).

How awesome to consider that the Creator of the galaxies and of time itself knows each one of us intimately. He knew each of us before we were born. He knew what we would look like; He knew our names; He knew for what purpose He had created us.

Just as the potter decides to make a vase or a cup or a plate from the lump of clay on the wheel, so God decides for what purpose He will make each of His vessels. Our God is not a capricious artist, randomly shaping his pots. Our God is a Potter who shapes us with great care and thought. Our God is a Potter who knows beauty and harmony, order and symmetry. Our God is a

Potter who finishes a vessel and asserts, "This is my vessel; it is very good!"

[2]

As the potter sits at the wheel to begin his work of shaping the clay, he is the master; the clay need only respond to the movement of his hands. The clay has no work to do in its own power; it must only follow the hands of the potter. Following is so important.

In life as well as in the clay, the quiet ability to follow, to cooperate, may be the inherent key to success. Our response is what counts—our response to the Word of God and our response to what we have been given. Is not the manner in which we use our income as important as the size of our income? Is not the way we live our lives as important as where we live? "Whoever can be trusted with very little can also be trusted with much, and whoever is dishonest with very little will also be dishonest with much" (Luke 16:10).

It is our glorious duty, then, to accept the cup that we have been given and to use it for all it is worth. Formed by the Master Potter, we need not complain if we have been given a mole or a freckle or a nose unlike our neighbor's. Our complaining about the way the Potter has made us is a serious affront.

But who are you, O man, to talk back to God? "Shall what is formed say to him who formed it,

'Why did you make me like this?' " Does not the potter have the right to make out of the same lump of clay some pottery for noble purposes and some for common use? (Romans 9:20–21).

Let us call a halt to that sort of self-punitive attitude and declare a silent resolution to the world and to ourselves:

"I believe I am the workmanship of my Potter's hands. There is none other like me in all the land. I am a chosen vessel of the King of Kings; I am unique; I am special; I am individual. I am who I am, and I accept myself with all of my limitations and all of my possibilities. And I ask God day by day, in the name of Jesus, to help my unbelief."

The great *I Am* has fashioned each one of us, and in every person there is worth. Genuine self-worth is the opposite of false pride, which is a terrible sin committed primarily by people who try to compensate for their sin of downgrading and for their failure to respond to the fine qualities with which they have been endowed. Each of us must prize the uniquenesses that are ours; for God has made us, and He does not do poor work. We need to forgive—by first *deciding* to forgive—our own sins and past mistakes.

A friend and I were having tea together when she accidentally spilled her tea on the table. "I'm terrible; I can't do anything right," she said. That kind of statement is a lie, an unnecessary accusation that kills the inner self. It should be changed to state the truth that sets us free from the bonds of self-pity. The truth is simply, "I spilled a little tea. I can clean it up."

Our human nature wants us to inflict an extra lash of punishment by adding those awful, damaging phrases to ourselves and others. To the school girl who breaks a glass trying to help set the table, an impatient parent may say, "You can't do anything right! You'll never amount to anything." And with that kind of encouragement, she just might measure down to her parent's expectations.

We need to forgive ourselves for our past mistakes. God is aware of our sins and weaknesses; yet He loves us in spite of all of them. He knows that we are but dust. "For he knows how we were formed, he remembers that we are dust" (Psalm 103:14). But from that dust He made us who we are.

One of the most serious illnesses in the world today is depression. Doctors say there are two related causes: low self-esteem and failure to achieve unrealistic goals. The second seems to hinge on the first, for we set goals beyond our abilities because we have not accepted ourselves as we are. We have not valued ourselves with the worth the Creator has given us in calling us forth as one of His vessels. Let us affirm His creation and confess: "I am a vessel created by the Master Potter; therefore, I have worth." Let us be done with self-denigration, damaging remarks, and complaining.

The role of the clay is to accept the decision

of the potter and to receive his transforming design.

How often we human beings, unlike the silent clay, complain of our limitations and overlook the finer qualities we have been given. Have you ever envied someone for being more handsome than you? Have you ever wished you were more talented in a certain area than you are? Have you ever tried to do something you were not prepared to do because deep inside you wanted to be like someone else who could do that thing well? Stop looking at others and be yourself. Wherever you are on the road of life, you are in the process of becoming the unique person God wants you to be. All of us are on the way to becoming more, and none of us has arrived yet.

"Oh, if only I could know the will of God for my life," many Christians say. "If only I could be like that person over there." We imagine ourselves in some future role, or we lament where we are today. But the will of God may require that we be right where we are on the path we are traveling at this moment. The Potter does not hurry His clay, and the clay cannot hurry the Potter.

If we want to know and do God's will, we must first accept ourselves and then be receptive to change. From then on He will continually and gradually change us. His will is revealed in stages, as demonstrated by the generating of the clay pot. Seldom does anyone see all of God's will at once. We see only so far, and we know only so much.

Then as we use what He has given us already, we are enabled to move into new frontiers and more revelation. Spiritual maturity comes one day at a time, and we need not be discouraged if we see ourselves as only a lump sitting on the Potter's wheel while all around us there are full-grown vessels.

Wherever we are in the Potter's process, He will be with us. "Have I not commanded you? Be strong and courageous. Do not be terrified; do not be discouraged, for the LORD your God will be with you wherever you go" (Joshua 1:9). If we are a solid chunk on the wheel, He wants to lift us taller and make us open on the inside. Whatever shape He gives us on the outside depends on how open He can make us on the inside. He wants us to be open to fresh thinking and worthy appraisal of the possibilities we have to offer.

Cicero said, "To think is to live." But a lot of people think so little of themselves that the saying could be reversed, "To think is to die." Marcus Aurelius said, "Your life is what your thoughts make it."

The Potter, who is God Himself, wants us to be open to beautiful thoughts, loving thoughts, acceptable thoughts. Therefore, we must determine to stop tearing ourselves down and let God make us better than we were yesterday.

Pious people of little faith say, "Oh, if only I could learn to be myself and nothing more." Godly men and women of burning faith say, "Oh, if only I could learn to be myself and nothing less."

A few years ago I had real difficulty accepting myself. I felt that all the people around me were better than I was and were living more exalted and honorable lives than I was. They did not do anything to make me feel this way; it was an inner struggle with myself. I found myself surrounded by missionaries, pastors, Christian leaders, and church workers, while I was just an ordinary person working in the world, making egregious mistakes along the way. I saw myself as a commoner among accredited associates. They had been to Bible school; I had not. I could only be a writer reporting what others were doing, or perhaps a teacher in a secular school helping students grow up to fill noble ranks that would tower over me.

Just as my self-image was at its lowest ebb, I picked up my little oar, a cheap ball-point pen, and wrote this parable about self-esteem.

That's What I Am, A Pear Tree

I produce pears. That's what I am, a pear tree, a manufacturer of simple yellow-green pears, year after year.

One day I looked to my right and there was a tree not half as tall as I, but jeweled with rubylike, luscious fruit. Apples, they were. For some reason, I had gotten stuck in an apple orchard. As far as I could see—and being pretty tall, I could see pretty far—there were rows and rows of apples trees with their red jewels glistening in the sun.

I didn't know how I got here. Perhaps in some little boy's pocket that had a hole in it ten, twenty years ago. Or maybe a sparrow spit me out along the way or dropped me in the dust and couldn't find me again and the dirt covered me over. But I looked at me, and I looked at them, those apple trees crowned with glorious red. And there I was, with my gangling height and my pea-green offspring. Who am I? I cried. Red is beautiful and green is not. Wherever I looked, wherever I turned, red was the life that oozed from the earth.

Nobody ever laughed at me, but someone always pointed and looked up as if wondering why I was not yielding the same red apples as my colleagues. They *were* my colleagues, those apple trees; I just didn't know it yet. And they seemed so busy and full of themselves that they hadn't noticed me, I was sure.

Then one day I looked down at my feet, and I saw—we were kindred after all. For the apple that fell and was left to rot upon the ground was the same brown as the fallen pear. And I marveled at the sameness: that in the dying, both are brown. And from the death of each, came life—but only then. And green was each plant that sprang from the earth, and green the leaf of both apple and pear.

I lifted my limbs, I clapped my leaves, and I whispered a rustling praise; for the God I know is the God they know—I am a misfit no longer, no. For I produce pears. That's what I am, a pear tree.

I thought I heard from the cloud above, "Submit, submit." From the worm that crawled below, "Submit, submit." From the storms that blew, "Submit, submit." In the drenching rain I was all but drowned, yet the message was all the same. Submit to this, submit to that. Until I clung one day to a thundering voice: "STAND. RISE UP." And I stretched forth my withered hand. For I produce pears. That's what I am, a pear tree!"

i am
In the image of the great I AM.
Praise God, I am who I am, and nothing less!

Forming the Vessel

"I am fearfully and wonderfully made" (Psalm 139:14).

A child watched his father in the basement of their home as the man chipped away at a block of white marble that he had purchased in Italy. Weeks passed, and the father often worked late into the night while the boy was not watching. Finally one morning the sculptor took his son by the hand and led him to the covered piece on which he had been working. He lifted the cloth, and there sat a solid white statue of Abraham Lincoln. The sculptor's son clapped his hands to his mouth in great surprise. "Father!" he shrieked. "How did you know he was in there?"[9]

Teachers, military officers, mothers and fathers,

coaches, company managers, and ministers are like the sculptor who knew someone important was in there. All hold within them a power to stimulate others to achieve, grow, work, progress, and become more than they were yesterday.

In sculpting, however, the object is achieved by taking away something, such as chiseling stone or carving wood, ice, or soap. In pottery, on the other hand, the whole lump of clay is transformed into a vessel. As the potter works directly with his hands to guide the formless to the formed, there is no reduction of the basic element.

Most art techniques require one of three types of action: adding, taking away, or making a negative. Building a house involves taking materials and adding them a bit at a time until the form appears. Weaving cloth, stringing beads, making a cake, writing a book, painting a landscape—all are accomplished by adding a little at a time. Sculpting, as I have mentioned, involves a process of taking away. And photography, as well as casting metals, involves making a negative, which is actually a completed version of the opposite form.

We can see aspects of the Creator in all of these, but it is the work of the potter that provides the clearest picture of the work of God in our lives. Without destroying any part of us, the Master Potter softens us and transforms us, bends us and shapes us. Pottery making is not a reformation; it is a transformation.

Gradualness is the heart of the transformation

process and the key to the human process. The goal of the potter is to bring the completely finished vessel off the wheel in the desired shape, with the proper toughness—a useful vessel, identifiably the work of the master potter but serving those who may not have ever met the potter.

The process of becoming more than we were yesterday—that is, entering the will of God—may be as gradual as the generating of the clay form. Hence the pot that is half-formed and gradually moving into its final dimensions is no less in the will of God than the beautiful teapot that has been serving for years.

[2]

The Potter does not push and pull us aimlessly. Like a mother urging her moist, newborn infant from the womb, the Potter uses every rhythm and every muscle, pushing, urging, stretching, exerting much labor to bring each of His vessels into the world individually. The Potter has chosen us as His clay and purified us; He has conditioned us. He has patiently left us to rest undisturbed for a number of days, and just before He positions us on the wheel to center us, He takes us from our rest and exercises us one more time. He kneads us and kneads us and kneads us.

Insufficient kneading will cause the clay to fail at the wheel, and too much kneading is not only a waste of time, but may be damaging as well. Only the experienced potter knows when his clay has had enough, for he knows what he is trying to accomplish by the kneading process.

The clay is kneaded primarily for three reasons: air pockets and bubbles in the clay have to be driven out; if the clay has hardened at all during the resting period, it is necessary to add water and knead the clay until it is the proper consistency for final working; and kneading equalizes the moisture content throughout the clay.

If air pockets are allowed to remain, the air will expand rapidly during firing and cause an explosion, spoiling the whole piece of work. If water content is unequally distributed, the clay will shrink unequally during firing and the piece will become warped. Kneading helps eliminate these dangers and reduces the tendency rested clay has to stick to the hands. Kneading equips the clay for its independence, the same as discipline and training enable children to enter adulthood or students and trainees to enter their profession.

It does not take a long study of clay for us to recognize a little about our human character. But if we want to know something of the character of God, we should try kneading a lump of clay.

Among Asian potters and their apprentices, it is said that it takes three years to learn how to knead clay, to learn how the hands must move, how the clay should feel when it is ready, and how the potter and his clay work together as one. "The clay not only needs the potter's pushing; it also requires his support," a potter told me. He said the potter learns to work with the tenderness and fragility of the clay rather than its toughness. He must follow the nature of his clay as well as lead it.

Beginners tend to rely too much on applying force to the clay when they are kneading it; as a result, they soon discover that the clay will not react as they want or that it sticks to the kneading board. Once they learn that rhythm, not force, is the key, they discover that the clay behaves in an interesting and satisfactory fashion.

Business executives and personnel managers observe the same results in their dealings with people. Husbands and wives find that gentleness and mutual support yield the best results in their relationships. Pastors learn that the church responds more favorably to encouragement and support than to pressure alone.

The kneading process is ultimately a process of freeing the clay. But the freedom the potter hopes for his clay is not one that lets it do whatever it wants to do; rather, it is a freedom that equips the clay to be able to do what it needs to do. The ballerina, the skater, the musician, the gymnast, the linguist—all have gone through rigorous discipline—kneading—that frees them and that enables them to do what they need to do.

For the clay to retain its shape when it is dry, the potter carefully balances kneading with rest. In a new book on the care of the human heart, I noticed the same balance. Topping a list of instructions for a healthy heart was, "Take enough time for exercise," and right beneath it, "Take enough time for rest."

A cake must not taste of egg in one bite, sugar in another, or flour in yet another; but as one whole it must blend all ingredients into a tasty consistency. Just as the cook beats and folds the batter before baking it, so the potter works his clay through and through.

Similarly, God as our Potter works us through and through to blend love and understanding, endurance and determination, sensitivity and kindness, all the many flavors of our personality and character.

[3]

Wherever there is a flaw, the clay itself is powerless to correct it. Wherever there is a flaw the clay can improve only by giving in to the potter's method of restoration. That is the crux— the potter's method of restoration. People stumble on this point.

The Bible says, "You will know the truth, and the truth will set you free" (John 8:32). But many people want freedom without truth. They want restoration, but they reject the Potter's method of restoration. They want eternal life, but they do not want Jesus Christ who is the only way to eternal life.

The restoration process starts at Base One: "All have sinned and fall short of the glory of God" (Romans 3:23). Most people who reject the gospel after hearing it, reject it not because of their unbelief but because of their refusal to admit that they have sinned. They reason away their sin. They reject the truth that sin is sin whether everybody does it or not. They reject the truth that all have sinned. They reject the truth that "the wages of sin is death, but the gift of God is eternal life in Christ Jesus our Lord" (Romans 6:23).

The most powerful sentence in the English language is, without a doubt, "I made a mistake." Those words can restore human relationships; they can restore health. Hospitals, both for the physically ill and the mentally ill, would not be nearly so full today if people could utter those words and start at Base One. Then, Base Two would follow: "If it is true that I need Jesus to be restored, then I will call on Him, and He will lead me as the potter leads his clay."

The touch of Jesus on His clay is a steady work between inner and outer forces. As He knows the inner life of the clay, the Potter knows both what it can do and what it will not do.

[4]

In the wedging and kneading the potter senses his material, takes possession of it, and begins to develop a rapport with it. It is the start of action toward making the intended vessel. When he has sufficiently wedged the clay, it is ready for forming.

The potter wets the center of the wheel slightly with water, to provide adhesive strength, and throws a ball of clay onto the spot. (If the wheel is made of plaster, it starts damp; the wheel made of wood or metal starts dry.) He then shapes the clay into a cone, patting the base of the mound as he rotates the wheel at a fast speed to force the clay to center and remain firm.

Here the potter tames his clay; that is, he stops any tendencies it might have to behave erratically. To tame his clay, he grips it firmly in both hands and pulls it upward. As soon as he has pulled it up, he puts his hands on top of the clay and presses it downward again with the wheel in motion, as if to remind his clay that the hand of the potter is in control and not the movement of the wheel upon which it revolves.

Then he pulls the clay into a cone shape once more, cupping his hands and *collaring* it upward with much force. These two movements—pulling upward, knocking down, and pulling upward again—are the potter's stretching techniques.

As our Master Potter, God stretches us, His vessels. Many of us have been lifted up to a peak experience, only to find ourselves knocked flat. "I was at a peak, right on the verge of success," we say. "Why am I put down again?" But if we see the clay as a picture of ourselves, we can recognize our personal come-downs not as regression but as progression, as a stretching process and a step toward greater heights. Such is the mastery of life. "And we know that in all things God works for the good of those who love him, who have been called according to his purpose" (Romans 8:28).

Putting his left thumb in the center of the top of the cone of clay on the rotating wheel, the potter applies pressure gradually. (In America it is generally the left hand inside and right hand outside, but in Japan it is the right hand inside with the left hand on the outside, depending on whether the rotation of the wheel is clockwise or counter-clockwise.)

Slowly he thins and raises the walls of the pot he is forming by pulling his thumb toward the palm of his left hand. The concave opening in the top of the clay must be opened gradually. If this opening is hurried, the concavity will be off-center and the clay will tear.

The potter wields tremendous force in this early stage of the vessel's development. With pressure, determination, and persistence he slowly hollows the little cone in his hands and begins to give it identity. Until this moment its only name was "clay," just as a baby is simply "the baby" until the day a name is given and that name becomes the person's identity for life.

But the hollowed-out clay is only the beginning of identity. Together the hollow and the cylindrical sides must be raised and made to grow into a pot. The principal difficulty in cylinder making or in making any form on the wheel, for that matter, is the tendency of the clay not to rise. Potters say it is one of their most frustrating moments, because the clay has a natural tendency to squat down where it is.

People have the same tendency to resist change. We often stop short of the mark. We attain a little foreign language ability, but we do not persist until we have enough fluency to really communicate in that language. We gain a little knowledge of the Bible, but we resist the discipline that it takes to master the Scriptures so that we can grasp their meaning for our day-to-day conflicts. We develop a little musical ability, but we are not willing to do the hard work that it takes to become an accomplished musician. Sometimes our resistance is really fear—fear of the thing we really want to do. The student who has a chance to study abroad or the person who comes up for a job promotion, while desperately wanting the new challenge, admits to a pounding heart and an inner fear of taking the jump.

Many Christians rest comfortably in their salvation and their position in a church but tend, like the clay, not to go on to higher service. We fall into complacency, even if a restless complacency, and have to be nudged onward by some force.

Interestingly, the final thrust to move upward comes from the force of the potter *inside* the pot instead of from an external influence.

Within this tendency of the clay not to rise, the cylinder has a tendency to spread outward into a bowl-like shape rather than be narrowed vertically. Verticality has to be restored by the potter's dominating left hand and fingers on the inside that narrow the circumference and collar the clay tightly upward. Having been pushed and stretched, opened and expanded, the clay has to be narrowed and restrained to give it identity as a vase, a jar, or a tea pot. It now begins to take on the fine lines that give it worth.

The observer sees only the outer vessel taking shape. The potter sees the space inside being expanded, limited, and taking form as if by the drawing of lines. The late Shoji Hamada said that the potter is an interior artist working from inside out, as nearly one with his clay as he knows how to be.

The Master Potter knows us intimately. As He produces necessary changes in our lives or in the lives of others, we only see the changes as they appear on the outside. But the Lord is really at work changing the shape of the inner person as the Holy Spirit shapes and molds our inner selves. The results of the inner changes are not always readily seen in the outward expression of our lives, but the Potter knows what He is doing. He knows in what direction He is taking us.

For us to take shape, the Potter sometimes needs to use forceful action. But at the same time that He is forcefully shaping us, He is also giving us support and stability. Instead of resisting the force of God, we need to trust Him as our Potter and know that the hand that uses pressure to shape us also holds us up and gives us support.

The work between inner and outer forces is enacted by the potter's two hands. The left hand, in charge of the inside, expresses and defines the pot's space and capacity to contain. The right hand, pressing from the outside, controls, directs, and defines the pot's form. The left hand pushes outward in a rather generalized gesture, while the right hand furnishes the focus and the proportion.

These two forces at work in a pot—inside-outside, left hand–right hand, space-contour, swelling-constriction—are like God at work in our lives through inner aspirations, desires, and needs and through outer circumstances, situations, and positions. Inside and outside, we are His design.

When the potter pulls his clay as it whirls on the wheel, he never starts near the top nor in the middle of the cylinder. Each pull starts at the bottom and continues all the way to the top. Each pull begins at the base to include the total piece.

Before he was raised up to lead a nation of three million people from a land of slavery into a new land of freedom, Moses was brought down to become a shepherd for forty years. Some have remarked that it was a waste for a military genius like Moses to spend all those years herding sheep in a wilderness. And yet what better preparation for the greater task of herding three million human wanderers across the wilderness? We cannot teach what we do not know, and we cannot lead where we have not been. Thus, what better preparation could Moses have had to lead God's people around the dark crevices and through the parching desert, than to have been thrust out to fight for his own survival in that wilderness?

When the Potter brings us down and starts us from the bottom again, it is always for a higher purpose. His shaping method makes us stronger and surer vessels than we were before.

The master potter knows his clay, and too rapid an ascent will create a *spiral screw* in the cylinder every time, causing trouble in the next pull. Too rapid an ascent may cause the cylinder to lean instead of continue heading upward; it may cause the wall on one side to become too thin while the other is too thick. Distortion is bound to result.

On the other hand, too slow an ascent will bring the clay nowhere. The clay will become soggy and heavy.

Plenty of water must be used before each pull. With a sponge, the potter dribbles just enough water on the rim to spread over both the inside and the outside surface but not puddle excessively in the bottom or on the wheel head. Each pull is a separate operation. Between pulls, water is applied and the wheel is sped up. As the walls of the piece are thinned and the form is extended, the potter diminishes the speed.

The acceleration or deceleration of the wheel, the wetting, the pulling up, and the rim control will vary with the nature and size of the pot. What the pot looks like has little to do with the process. What counts is the feel of the turning clay and its subtle changes that are felt through the potter's fingers. Ideally, the potter feels the pot growing in his hands as the cylinder almost rises by itself at this point. A light, tender touch on the clay and a feeling of response tells the potter what is happening in the pot, and only he can really understand it.

The cylinder cannot be forced into existence; rather, it grows as a result of gentle collaboration between the potter's hands and his clay. Each cylinder will rise to a certain point; no further pull will cause it to rise higher. The clay seems to know when to stop so that the potter can bend and shape its delicate curves and lines. Then the potter caresses his clay gently but deliberately into the desired shape and smoothness.

[5]

The potter's wheel, the potter's chief creative tool, is one of the oldest mechanical devices known, dating back to at least 2000 B.C. The principle of the wheel itself speaks of repetition. Only as the lump of clay is turned around and around is it made to take on usefulness and identity. The potter could certainly make a pot without a wheel, but through the repetitious turning the vessel is made smooth, balanced, and even.

The sovereign Potter, Jesus, prepares us through the repetition of our day-to-day routine. Through the mundane, repetitious events of our lives, He spins us into a new shape, He lifts us higher than we were, and He spends all the time it takes to get us ready to serve in His kingdom. He corrects us along our journey, sensing our trouble spots; but He leaves our unique differences, accepting us for the total of what we are.

We are put into certain circumstances so that God can work out a perfecting work in us. The word "circumstances" itself is derived from the very circle, the wheel, that the potter works upon. The Latin root *circum* means "around," and *stance* means "to stand." Those who will *stand in the circle* of routine will surely come out refined and strengthened vessels, pleasing both Maker and observer.

But we need not stay forever in that routine that the Potter uses for forming us. We need not stay on the wheel, though we ourselves cannot leap from our position on the wheel. Nor can we be pushed off, lest in the landing we become marred and twisted, unfit for use. It is the Potter, and only the Potter, who is able to take His chosen vessel off the wheel. For He knows both when and how each one must be carefully yet forcefully cut loose.

[6]

I once saw a potter use an exciting technique for shaping his vessels: he breathed into the clay form, placing his mouth on the mouth of the bottle and blowing gently. The soft clay of the bottle gave under the pressure of the warm air and expanded lightly like a balloon.

This stretching and extension can sometimes make a perfunctory form miraculously come alive. Pressure from within supplies what may have been lacking before—a sense of the inside, a positive feeling of interior space. Flat places in the form are blown out and the curves of the profile are unified and brought together.

Another technique used by some potters is that of closing in the bottle form entirely, trapping the breath inside. The air trapped inside gives an amazing resistance and springiness to the form, which then can be raised to a narrower shape or pushed down to a smaller shape without collapsing because the breath is inside. Later a new opening is made.

Breath itself is the spirit of every being. The first book of the Bible shows God making Adam from the clay and then breathing into him the breath of life. The first historical book after the death of Jesus shows the Holy Spirit coming like a breath of new power into the lives of His followers.

When God breathes upon us and fills us with His Holy Spirit, we, too, miraculously come alive.

94

The Holy Spirit within us provides the internal pressure or force that aids God in shaping us.

Having been carefully and skillfully formed, each vessel goes through a touching-up process. After these finishing stages, the vessel is ready for the ultimate test, the *maturing* action of the firing kiln.

> "I am fearfully and wonderfully made. . . . Search me, O God, and know my heart; test me and know my anxious thoughts. See if there is any offensive way in me, and lead in the way everlasting" (Psalm 139:14, 23–24).

PART THREE

The Potter Matures the Clay

Restoring the Vessel
Firing the Vessel
Celebrating the Vessel

Even as the fire changes the clay into pottery, certain elements in life that may be abrasive to us are at work refining us and profoundly transforming us to a more usable state.

Restoring the Vessel

"Behold, all things are become new" (2 Corinthians
5:17 KJV).

Before removing the pot from the wheel, the
potter examines it for flaws. He checks it for balance: Is one side of the pot thinner than the other?
He checks it for shape: Is the neck of the vase
centered or lopsided? He checks it for deformities:
Is the lip of the pitcher correctly positioned? He
checks it for nicks or ridges left by his wooden
shaping tool.

The potter sometimes allows a flaw to remain
and uses it to enhance the individuality and unique-
ness of the vessel. Sometimes he may reshape the
pot or reform a crooked neck. And other times he

may find that the pot needs complete restoration, which he does by collapsing the wet pot into a lump and starting over from the beginning.

We are often like the potter's vessels—lopsided, out of balance, deformed, scarred by nicks. We live in a world marred by sin, and as a result we live with illnesses, birth defects, violence, and tragedy. Although God is not the author of sin, He has allowed His creation to live with the consequences of its sin and rebellion against His ways.

How do we respond to these imperfections in our lives? How do we cope with our flaws? Again, we can gain insight from the potter and the clay.

Water pots made by Maria and Julian Martinez have bottoms that are arched inward. By cultural standards other than those of the Pueblo, such an arch in pottery might be a nuisance or even a deformity. But Maria shaped her pots to facilitate carrying them on the head. In their unique way they are perfect. What appears to some people to be a weakness or imperfection in the Martinezes' water pots is actually an important quality in their function and use.

Certain bowls and tea cups made in Japanese potteries have a distinct V-shaped notch on the base. I have observed prospective buyers from the city picking up the cups and turning the notch to the wall, rummaging in vain to find a set unblemished by the little notch. Yet that notch is a safeguard against breakage in shipment. For shipment the cups and bowls are stacked into one another with straw between and then tied with cord. The top bowl in the set is turned upside down on the stack and the string is secured in the V-shaped notch. It is not a flaw, but a mark cut by the potter to serve a definite purpose.

When judged by appearance, these pots and cups are thought to be inferior. Yet when we look beyond the outward appearance of these vessels, we understand their use and function and see how valuable they are. The flaws make them unique; and what at first glance appeared to be a weakness is actually a strength that gives the vessels meaning and purpose.

When we look at ourselves and at others and begin to judge by outward, physical characteristics, let us go again to the potter's house. What may appear to be a flaw or weakness may actually be a strength. Ability and worth are not determined by what we see as the outer person. What to the insensitive eye may appear as a physical clumsiness does not in any way suggest mental or spiritual clumsiness. The incompetence lies neither in the Potter nor the vessel; the incompetence lies in others' ignorance and unwillingness to look beyond what is external to the inner worth and value of a person.

The Old Testament reveals the Master Potter's standard of judgment. His eye sees far beyond our outward appearance and behavior. The wisdom that shapes us far exceeds our understanding.

When Samuel needed to choose a king to rule

over Israel, he was impressed by one man in particular. "But the LORD said to Samuel, 'Do not consider his appearance or his height, for I have rejected him. The LORD does not look at the things man looks at. Man looks at the outward appearance, but the LORD looks at the heart'" (1 Samuel 16:7).

"'For my thoughts are not your thoughts, neither are your ways my ways,' declares the LORD. 'As the heavens are higher than the earth, so are my ways higher than your ways and my thoughts than your thoughts'" (Isaiah 55:8).

[2]

Although a person's life might be marred in some way, all that is marred is not useless. Thomas Edison went deaf when he was a young man, but he didn't allow that handicap to stop him. He went on to invent the light bulb, one of more than a thousand of his electrical inventions that have brought light and power for millions throughout the world. Hermit, inventor, philosopher, the jovial Edison may have indeed been improved rather than impaired by his affliction. His deafness may have enabled him to think better, to exclude outside distractions. In silence he was able to get on with that which burned inside him to be accomplished. His deaf condition even spared him hearing the ridicule of unbelieving friends. His genius was allowed to germinate and grow in the protective incubator of silence.

Beethoven was completely deaf, unable to hear his own music performed. Helen Keller was a deaf-mute. Ethel Waters was a child born out of rape to a twelve-year-old mother. Had she been conceived today, she would no doubt have been aborted on government funds and the world would not have known her mellow voice praising her Creator with "His Eye Is on the Sparrow."

Although each of these men and women lived with a major imperfection, they did not allow that imperfection to render them useless people. Each of them lived a full life *in spite of* his or her handicap and *because of* that handicap.

Pottery takes on a surface texture resulting from the movement at the wheel, and this surface becomes as much a part of the final pot as either the form or glaze. There might be impressions of the potter's hand both inside and out. The wooden *rib* he uses as a smoothing tool may leave a slight streak on the exterior of the pot. The string or wire that he holds taut when cutting the infant pot from the mother lump of clay may leave a rippling or circular design on the flat bottom of the vessel.

The potter could trim away all such marks that mar his pot. And yet all mars, all scars, all impressions are not necessarily unbefitting. Rather than erase them, he sometimes chooses that they should stay to withstand the fire and adorn the vessel permanently. If left, they are part of the potter's will, and not some oversight that caught him unaware.

As a teenager Joni Eareckson was injured in a diving accident that left her a quadriplegic. Did these imperfections make her useless? Not at all. Joni's books, records, and paintings (done with pen or brush held in her mouth) reveal a joyful woman whom God has powerfully used. Through her own struggles with quadriplegia, Joni Eareckson Tada has established a ministry that helps churches meet the needs of physically handicapped persons.

Miura Ayako, one of Japan's Christian novelists, was bedridden with tuberculosis for a decade. Her spine was damaged, and her body was weakened for life. Yet in one short lifetime she has done more to perpetuate good and shine the light of biblical truth on a national level than perhaps any other person in that country.

After a suicide attempt, Yoneko Tahara was left with one arm, three fingers, and no feet; yet the Master Potter reshaped her thoughts and turned her around in His loving hands. Then He paired her up with a man who loved her, and the Tahara family has brought inspiration and meaning to thousands of others groping for hope in a meaningless world.

All that is marred is not useless. The Master Potter has used these marred vessels—along with many others—to touch a multitude of lives for Himself. God has not only used them *despite their flaws;* He has also *used the flaws* to glorify Himself.

Through lives such as these He clearly demonstrates that all things—even flaws, imperfections, tragedies—work together for good to them that love God and are called according to His purpose (Romans 8:28 KJV).

[3]

The potter is sovereign. When he discovers that one of his vessels on the wheel needs reshaping or reforming, he can use a variety of methods to restore it. The freshly made pot, still wet and soft, can be squeezed, pushed, carved, bent, expanded, added to, pinched for pouring, or even collapsed and started all over. When the newborn pot dries a little, the potter might impress a rope design on the sides or comb a checkered finish into the leatherlike clay. He might stick on a spout, a handle, ears, or other motifs, either knoblike or dainty and delicate; or he might leave it plain.

Whatever changes the potter makes to the form of the vessel, he makes while his pot is in motion. The whirling clay is the softest and the most responsive to his touch, just as the wheels of a car in motion are easier to turn than the wheels of a car that is parked or standing still.

I have observed that the same is true of human beings. Those who are already being worked, those who have already yielded and have been set in motion, are more responsive and more purposefully directed into functional and beautiful beings than those waiting on the sidelines until just the right opportunity suits their fancy.

One of the most effective pastors I know got his start by cleaning toilets and emptying trash. He did not continue those tasks forever, but doing them started him in motion. It was part of his routine at the wheel, and the Potter was able to give shape and refinement to the man in that willing condition.

Marion Anderson scrubbed steps, going door to door with a bucket and brush, shining people's steps on her hands and knees. At each job she earned a penny or an occasional nickel that she carefully saved to buy a violin she had seen for three dollars and forty-five cents in a pawn shop. Already set in motion, the aspiring singer, who was rejected by a school of music on the basis of her skin color, was chosen by the Potter for inner qualities that He alone could know; and in her willingness the Master Potter made of Marion Anderson a treasured singer whom the world would hear and applaud. Not destined forever to the routine of washing steps, she was nevertheless set in motion at such a level, and the Potter was thus able to change the formless to the formed, the same as He had changed the embryonic world of His creation from chaos to order. "And the earth was without form, and void; and darkness was upon the face of the deep. And the Spirit of God *moved* upon the face of the waters. And God said,

Let there be light: and there was light" (Genesis 1:2–3 KJV, italics mine).

Setting clay in motion, trimming, or smoothing clay in motion involves risk. It risks injury or defeat; it risks scars. But the movement is necessary, for only the clay that has been set in motion is pliable and workable. As the potter wields his tools during the routine turning of the wheel, he brings his vessel to a higher form of beauty and usefulness.

[4]

The potter knows what he is doing from the very beginning. He never mixes bad clay with the good, for good clay will never improve the bad; rather, the bad will render the mixture useless, completely useless. The potter knows what he must change, and he knows what he can remold. He knows how much his clay can take and how many times he can collapse it and form it again. He knows how much he can stretch it and how much he can bend it. Some vessels are marred to the extent that the potter needs to remake them completely.

The Bible pictures the potter as he reforms a misshapen pot: "This is the word that came to Jeremiah from the LORD: 'Go down to the potter's house, and there I will give you my message.' So I went down to the potter's house, and I saw him working at the wheel. But the pot he was shaping from the clay was marred in his hands; so the potter formed it into another pot, shaping it as seemed best to him" (Jeremiah 18:1–4).

I have watched the potter at the wheel as he took a terribly marred pot in his hands and changed its shape but not its substance. He started again with the same lump of clay on the wheel, spinning it round and round; but the second time he brought forth a new creation, clearly definable and perfect—what the potter wanted.

No matter how marred we become, the Master Potter can salvage us. None of us is beyond the restoring hand of the Lord. God is always willing to take our lives that have become misshapen by sin, abuse, and rebelliousness and reshape them, making us into new vessels of His choosing, *shaping as it seems best to Him.*

The Bible is full of men and women who needed a second chance. Moses killed a man, but God restored Moses and made him a dynamic and patient leader of an entire nation. Peter denied Jesus, but he returned to the Lord, and the Lord transformed him into a pillar of mighty strength in the church. Saul of Tarsus went about murdering and persecuting the very elect of God, but God Himself called Saul apart and gave him a second chance. When Saul responded to God's call and chose to believe that Jesus was the Christ, the Son of God, his life changed. The Potter transformed the murderous Saul into another vessel, the apostle Paul, of whom the Lord Jesus said, "He is a chosen vessel unto me, to bear my name before the Gentiles, and kings, and the children of Israel" (Acts 9:15 KJV). This restored vessel became a mighty Christian leader who wrote much of the New Testament and planted the Christian church as far away as Europe.

That kind of transformation is possible for anyone who will believe in Jesus Christ and co-operate with the ways of the Master Potter. The apostle Paul confirms this in one of his New Testament letters: "If any man be in Christ, he is a new creature: old things are passed away; behold, all things are become new" (2 Corinthians 5:17 KJV).

God is in the business of giving second chances, and the world we live in is filled with people in need of just that—another chance, a second try. The potter can lift up the clay that spiraled or went crooked and redeem it. That is what the Bible is all about. That is what life is all about.

The first Adam sinned, but Jesus, the second Adam, went about restoring men and women to that which they were meant to be. He straightened a man's withered hand. He released a man from evil spirits. He raised Lazarus from the dead. And when Lazarus came forth, bound hand and foot with graveclothes, Jesus commanded the people standing by: "Loose him, and let him go" (John 11:44 KJV).

These words, I think, epitomize the work of

Jesus: "Loose him, and let him go." He loosed people from their misshapen bondage. He dined with sinners. He said to the prostitute, "Go and sin no more." Like the potter, He went about giving a second chance to all who asked. The guilty listened to Jesus and began to see themselves as worthy vessels.

Who of us would not like to erase some image from our past and start all over? That is the kind of second chance God offers each of us, whoever we are, wherever we have fallen. Great or small, rich or poor, powerful or powerless, we are all fashioned out of clay—clay that can become marred along the way. Though some prefer to think they are made of better stuff, only statues are made of marble. And marble is cold, sad stuff, frozen forever in its form, without the breath of life, without ears to hear or voice to sing. Only God's chosen clay has within it the potential to change.

Being the Potter that He is, He can take you in His knowing hands, steady your trembling body, and fashion you again into a new work. Why don't you ask Him to do that for you today?

> "So the potter formed it into another pot, shaping it as seemed best to him" (Jeremiah 18:4).

Firing the Vessel

"But we have this treasure in jars of clay to show that this all-surpassing power is from God and not from us. We are hard pressed on every side, but not crushed; perplexed, but not in despair; persecuted, but not abandoned; struck down, but not destroyed" (2 Corinthians 4:7–9).

For many centuries women cut reeds from the grass and wove them into baskets. As they learned to sharpen flat stones and bamboo sticks, they were able to strip green bark from saplings and weave their baskets stronger and larger. In time they found that the clay soil that was too sticky for growing their corn was just right for lining their baskets. The clay would soften in their hands, and if their hands were wet enough, they could press the clay into the basket and it would hold that shape and dry as they left it.

The same stuff from which they formed adobe bricks to build their houses could be used to line their baskets to hold their grain. And the good sun would dry them both. For all their needs they depended on this antithesis of wet and dry, rain and sun; and in the absence of one, the other alone could be devastating.

One day a brush fire raged through the valley and the women left their baskets where they had been picking berries, grabbed their babies, and ran from the swirling smoke. Fire was sometimes friend and sometimes foe, the same as wind or fog or mist.

When the fire had burned out, the women took sticks and poked the ashes, looking for what might be left. Scattered in the smoldering embers they found clay baskets, deeper in color and stronger than anything their hands had made so far. The reeds had burned away but left their trace in the soot. All the berries were gone, but an indelible stain graced the inside walls of the clay forms that had turned to rock. When cooled, the clay baskets were able to hold not only grain but water.

There was magic in fire. It could turn ice to liquid or liquid to solids. It could purify a wound or destroy a village. It could turn clay to stone. The fire that cooked their hard foods soft and their soft foods crisp was the same fire that now gave them a new trade. They could make pots and trade them for shells and salt.

From beginnings such as these, fire was tamed, and pottery came to be baked in bonfires, caves, and open pits.

Without a wheel, the playful clay was pounded and pulled, coiled and pinched, smoothed and shaped into those vessels that would serve the needs of the people. Cooking utensils came into being and ovens were perfected. Earth, air, water, and fire, the four great elements, had been coaxed into helping men and women build their civilizations.

From the brush fires of yesterday to the relatively new invention of the electric kiln, the ancient art of pottery making has lasted thousands of years. Indeed, pottery vessels have often outlasted cultures—cultures that have long since been destroyed by floods and famines, pestilence, earthquakes, and wars. And every vessel that survives owes its survival to the fire, for without fire a pot can never be completely finished.

Fire is the test of tests. It brings maturity. The kiln is the place where the potter matures his pots. Any pot that does not go through this phase of the potter's plan is too soft to be of any value; the pot that does not spend its time in the kiln has form, but no enduring worth or function.

Clay undergoes chemical and physical change in its various stages, but fire produces the most enduring change of all. By some mystery the chemical constituency of the clay form actually hardens into a rocklike vessel, and if the fire is hot enough, the thin glaze that has been *dipped* on is turned into a glassy surface, smooth and pleasing to the touch. At any stage before being fired, the clay can be soaked in water and made soft and pliable for molding again. Even the vessel that has been dried and baked by the sun can be soaked back to its original softness. But no pot that has withstood the fire can ever again be reduced by soaking. The fire turns clay into pottery.

We see ourselves in this stage of the vessel's development, too. For God, like the potter, uses the fire to mature, strengthen, and change us. The Bible often uses the image of fire to speak of God's purifying activity, as He refines and changes His people.

Isaiah speaks of God's chosen people Israel being tested in the furnace of affliction (48:10). The New Testament writers also pick up this theme. They write about God using the fire of affliction—trials, difficulties, adversities—to bring us to maturity and usefulness. No person who has endured the testing of fiery trials will ever be the same.

We often fear the fire because we know that fire produces heat, pressure, and pain; we know that fire has the potential to destroy us. But in the hands of a loving God, fire brings forth vessels of endurance and supreme value—beauty and strength from the ashes of adversity.

James reflects on the function of fiery trials: "Consider it pure joy, my brothers, whenever you face trials of many kinds, because you know that the testing of your faith develops perseverance. Perseverance must finish its work so that you may be mature and complete, not lacking anything" (1:2–4).

[2]

The potter chose his clay, conditioned it, tamed it, stretched it, named it, and formed it. When he sponged off the wet vessel and lifted it from the wheel, it was so delicate in its raw clay state that he had to handle it as gently as a father would pick up his newborn child. With a string held taut between his hands, the potter cut loose the newborn pot from the mother lump of clay, leaving a navel-like swirl where the cord had been. So impressionable was the clay, that at this point any change was possible. The slightest touch of a fingertip might leave an indentation.

Gray and unadorned, the pot in its raw state was shielded from the wind and set down to dry slowly and evenly.

Natural drying may take two weeks, depending on the thickness of the pot, the humidity, and other environmental conditions. Too fast an evaporation of water from the walls of the vessel might cause it to burst or crack, while too slow an evaporation or uneven drying might make the pot lopsided. In cold climates, the newly formed vessels have to be protected from freezing, a drastic condition that would break the pot. If warping or breakage occurs, the damaged pot in its raw clay state can be broken down and mixed again into a workable but formless lump of clay. Those forms that manage to dry to *leather-hard* specifications can go on to be carved or engraved and then *bisque fired* at a low temperature.

The potter takes great care in this first firing of the clay. Even though the clay pots have dried for weeks, they will still have moisture in them when they are placed in the kiln. The presence of this water in the clay is a potential danger to the pot, for when the kiln is fired, the water heats up and expands. If the expansion is too great, the pot will burst.

For this reason, the pots are placed in the kiln while it is cold, and the fire is kindled slowly. Potters say that their pots are not lost by the degree of the heat in the kiln but by the abrupt changes of temperature to which the pots are exposed before they are ready to endure them. Potters also say that the appearance of a pot has nothing to do with whether or not it will burst. The strong-looking pot with heavy, thick sides is as susceptible to breakage or is perhaps even more likely to explode than the weaker, more delicate pot because the heavy one has more water content and has to let off steam in the heating process. The experienced potter knows that the build-up of steam could cause the pot to explode, so he provides *blowholes* at the top of the kiln as a means for the steam to escape.

How like our heavenly Father is the potter. When we are experiencing the pressure from difficult circumstances or when we are tempted to give in to discouragement and defeat as we face adversity, the Bible tells us that "No temptation has seized you except what is common to man. And God is faithful; he will not let you be tempted beyond what you can bear. But when you are tempted, he will also provide a way out so that you can stand up under it" (1 Corinthians 10:13).

The fact that we must suffer or that we must be tested and tried does not give other people the right to impose that suffering. Since the fall of Adam and Eve there have been sufficient kilns in life without our adding fire to the fire. However, realizing that we are God's workmanship, we might accept the events of our lives as one of the means whereby His creative purposes for us are fulfilled. We might decide to be teachable instead of belligerent, thankful instead of arrogant. "For our light and momentary troubles are achieving for us an eternal glory that far outweighs them all" (2 Corinthians 4:17).

Throughout the Bible there appears the recurring idea that our trials in life are disciplinary steps to purify and strengthen character, that our sufferings serve to test our faith. However we view our given circumstances, one thing is undeniable:

refinement does come. "For you, O God, tested us; you refined us like silver" (Psalm 66:10).

This first firing, called the bisque firing, is not the only firing that the clay will undergo. The bisque firing is merely a preparatory firing. The clay is heated only to the intensity that will harden the surface so that it will accept the glaze.

After the bisque firing is completed, the pots are still fragile; the clay is flaky, much like the consistency of chalk, and it can be easily chipped or broken. The pots are not water-resistant at this point, and they stain readily. If they are used after this first firing, they could poison their contents.

The potter knows that before the vessel is ready for use, it must be glazed and subjected to an even hotter firing. The intense heat is necessary for the pot to become mature and complete. After the second time in the intense heat of the kiln, the glaze will harden and the pot will be water-resistant and sufficiently durable for use.

Sometimes we, too, endure the pressure and heat from difficult experiences only to find ourselves again in the furnace of affliction. We may be angry that we are in the heat again. Yet God in His wisdom allows us to undergo the intense heat of trials and difficulties, for it is through these trials that He transforms us from weak, changeable people into strong, useful vessels. After we withstand the pressure of extreme difficulty, we will emerge mature and complete, ready to serve.

118

[3]

After the pot has cooled from the bisque firing, it is glazed. The potter may choose a basic glaze or a slip, which is a clay pigment itself thinned down to a liquid. While the function of the glaze is to make each vessel impervious to the wine, water, soup, or tea that it may someday hold, the glaze also brings color to the gray, earthen pot.

The glazing process is a demonstration of the potter's faith, a deposit of his hope. When he applies the glaze to the brittle pot, he knows the finished color promises to be superior to anything his eye can see, but all glazes look the same when they are applied. All liquid glazes are dark gray or whitish until the pots are fired again. There is sameness in the glazes as long as they are immature; only in the fire do the pigments respond and dare to be themselves.

Beauty results from the fire. The colors— brown and green, *ochre,* persimmon red, slate, or blue—are released only by intense heat. A drab, chalky glaze is transformed to smooth glass. Like jade or sapphire or rubies that result from tremendously high temperatures in the belly of the earth, the glazed pottery that comes from the potter's kiln is a rare gem in contrast to its former state when it was freshly dug and washed down from the hill.

The Old Testament story of Job illustrates

how God uses the fires of testing to bring forth beauty. Job recognized that even though he himself did not always see God's presence in his suffering, God was in control. "He knows the way that I take; when he has tested me, I will come forth as gold" (Job 23:10). The Bible further notes that "the Lord blessed the latter part of Job's life more than the first" (Job 42:12).

Cited for his troubles and for the way he responded to his troubles, Job has been singled out as a man who suffered dearly. Many who hear about Job from the pulpit and from Sunday school classes remember nothing else about him except that he suffered. But like the potter who waits to open the kiln, let us stay with Job through the final chapter.

When we are first introduced to Job in chapter one, we learn that he was already a prominent and wealthy man. In fact, the Bible says that "he was the greatest man among all the people of the East" (Job 1:3). He owned seven thousand sheep, three thousand camels, five hundred yoke of oxen, and five hundred donkeys. Yet verse twelve of the final chapter mathematically verifies the tenth verse and tells us that in the end he had fourteen thousand sheep, six thousand camels, a thousand yoke of oxen, and a thousand donkeys—twice as much as he had before.

Although early in the book we read that all Job's children had died in a typhoon or tornado or what the Bible calls "a mighty wind" that caused the house to collapse on them, at the end of the story Job had again fathered seven sons and three daughters, the same number of children he had had before. But this time the Bible notes that his daughters were especially beautiful. "Nowhere in all the land were there found women as beautiful as Job's daughters" (42:15).

"After Job had prayed for his friends, the LORD made him prosperous again and gave him TWICE AS MUCH AS HE HAD BEFORE" (Job 42:10, emphasis mine). "He saw his children and their children to the fourth generation. And so he died, old and full of years" (42:16–17). What a blessing! What more could he have asked? Surely Job's own words came true: "I will come forth as gold" (23:10).

Not all suffering in the world is inflicted by the Potter. C.S. Lewis estimated that human wickedness accounts for eighty percent of human sufferings. "It is men, not God, who have produced racks, whips, prisons, slavery, guns, bayonets, and bombs," he wrote in *The Problem of Pain*. "It is by human avarice and human stupidity, not by the churlishness of nature, that we have poverty and overwork."[10]

On the other hand, God does bring about circumstances in which we can discover His best for us, and sometimes those circumstances may involve pain or suffering on our part. But, the Bible reminds us, the pain and suffering produce good results. "Now for a little while you may have had to suffer grief in all kinds of trials. These have come so that your faith . . . may be proved genuine and may result in praise and honor when Jesus Christ is revealed" (1 Peter 1:6–7).

Like the clay in the potter's kiln, we are not merely strengthened by the fiery trials of life—we are changed. The clay is transformed from a soft, textured vessel to slippery glassware resembling a valuable and precious stone. Let us not remember only hard times; but let us expect beauty to come out of human suffering even as loveliness comes from the potter's kiln.

[4]

The second firing, at a higher temperature, melts the glaze that has been applied to the bisque ware and either partially or wholly *vitrifies* the clay—that is, turns it into a sort of glass. Every resulting color and every resulting texture are not necessarily predictable. In fact, it is this unpredictable nature of firing that heightens hope and adds excitement to pottery making.

As the potter and his helper prepare for the second firing, they carefully *stack* the kiln with those pots chosen to go on to maturity. The kiln is not stacked haphazardly. The potter handles each pot individually, examining it as a whole—its size, shape, texture, and glaze. Only as he sees the pot as a whole can the potter best determine where he will place the pot in the kiln.

While pots with various glazes stand side by side in the kiln, what is the best firing for one group of ware may not be the best for another. The fuel, the rate of temperature increases, the oxygen flow and other factors depend on the kind of ware being put to the fire, on the size of the kiln, and the number of pots waiting to be fired.

Sometimes a firing may involve three or four thousand pots, but each one is handled individually and placed so that a desired amount of heat can reach all around it. Only then will the glaze come forth and the vessel be strong and whole.

The decoration of the pot is not separate from the rest of the pot any more than the emotions of a person are separate from that person's spirit or body or skin. The decorative glaze becomes merely a part of the whole of the pot. Those pots judged to be prize-winning vessels are not chosen because of their glaze or their outward appearance alone. They are chosen because of their wholeness—the intrinsic blend of form, function, proportion, movement, color, and texture.

Just as we sometimes miss the real value of a piece of pottery by our quickness to judge the glaze apart from its intrinsic relationship to the whole pot, we also miss the whole beauty of the people around us. We judge other people by their accomplishments or their names or their appearance alone. We must learn to see the whole person.

In 1890 the president of Tokyo University gave an address paying tribute to Niijima Jo, forty-seven, who had recently died. Niijima, the founder of Doshisha University in Kyoto and contributor of immeasurable good to the future of Japan, had discovered a friend's Bible during his youth and had been so impressed with what it said that he dared to become a stowaway on a ship to find a teacher in America who could tell him more about God. Though the Bible was a forbidden book in Japan in those days and there was not one in his own language, Niijima had read his friend's Chinese translation in secret. "My prince beated me," he related, "and friends laughed me."

Upon discovering God, he determined the course of his life from that day forward: "I must run into His ways!"[11] Running then from Japan's isolationism when the country was closed to outside education on any subject in any form, Niijima Jo left his samurai-class family and the shores of Japan at the risk of his life. He sold his swords to buy a New Testament for eight dollars in Shanghai and went through bitter hardships to learn English and study in America. Niijima had one aim in view—to translate the Bible into Japanese and teach his fellow Japanese the ways of Christ as the means of salvation and eternal life. Niijima saw Christianity as the means of improving his whole country at its core and thereby making it a peaceful and prosperous nation that would combine morality with freedom.

Of all the speakers at the memorial service that day in 1890, only the president of Tokyo

University, Hiroyuki Kato, was not a Christian. He had greatly admired Niijima Jo, but President Kato missed the wholeness of the man's life. In his remarks about Niijima, President Kato said, "I do not praise him because he was a Christian. I care not whether he believed in Jesus or not. I praise him for that steadfast spirit, so essential in every sphere. . . . We are a clever people. . . . It is a good thing to be clever, but to be clever only is to lack strength. Cleverness and steadfastness of purpose rarely go hand in hand. The former is apt to taper away into shallowness and fickleness, and the fickle, shallow mind can rarely carry through to its end any great undertaking. . . . In the case of Mr. Niijima, however, from the very first, when he decided to go to America, to the close of his life, this invincible spirit was conspicuous."[12]

What Kato had failed to recognize, however, was the Source of that spirit or steadfastness that he so greatly admired and that he acknowledged was missing in most people. The essence of Niijima's greatness was his belief in Jesus, the very portion of Niijima that Kato said he did not care about. He may as well have removed the man's heart or his liver as to try to separate Niijima Jo from that faith that made him what he was. Niijima could not be dissected and removed from his love of God. *It was that very portion of him that made the rest of him possible!* Can we scrape the glaze from a clay vessel and call those pigments beautiful while destroying the vessel that the glaze rested upon?

"I am no more my parents', but my God's," Niijima had written in a letter many years before. "I must serve my Heavenly Father more than my earthly parents. *This new idea gave me courage* to make a decision to forsake my prince, and also to leave my home and my country temporarily." (italics mine)[13]

Niijima never intended to leave Japan permanently, and he never intended to study without studying God. It was for the purpose of lifting Japan from her immorality of that era that he hid himself and escaped to study: and it was for the purpose of studying God to which all his studies were directed. It was for the one purpose of teaching the Christian faith that the famous Doshisha University was founded, the name itself meaning "the one-purpose company."

Almost a century has passed since the burial of Niijima Jo. But one hundred years later, while the name Hiroyuki Kato is nearly unknown, the name Niijima Jo brings a glimmer of admiration and recognition throughout the nation: "Oh, yes, I know him. He was a great Christian!" Niijima is defined by the faith that compelled him, the very cause that outlasted the body that contained him.

Kato made a mistake. A person's courage cannot be separated from the Source that gives that courage, any more than a clay jar can be separated from its chemistry. The essence of us all cries out

126

for acceptance of our wholeness, the *substance* of who we are because of all that we are.

With an eye for their wholeness, the potter chooses where to place each pot in the kiln. Certain glazes benefit by more intense, direct heat; others need the shadow of large pots nearby to shield them a little; and some are placed inside already fired containers to lighten the effect of the heat. While the potter protects certain pots from the carbon and ash that result from the natural action of the kiln, he positions others to receive maximum treatment from such natural glazing as the flames can perform.

The kiln that burns wood as fuel provides both great risk and adventure to the glaze on the pots. The carbon content as well as the sparks from the fire mix with the glazes and put an interesting surface effect on the natural clay as the flames react with the mineral content of each glaze.

It is significant that the potter does not toss the pots into the kiln and leave them unattended. Not only does he see that they are stacked carefully, but he also sits on watch through the duration of the firing or leaves someone in charge who knows what to do. Whether they be the large eight-chamber kilns in Mashiko or the small one-chamber kilns, the kilns are stoked at regular intervals for forty-two hours straight by the men who keep watch through the night. Like angels positioned along the outer walls of the kiln, they do more than watch; they slow down the action of the first chamber or increase intensity in the last one. At times the stoking becomes a vigorous job, but regular and rhythmic are the powerful movements of the arms that rapidly and forcefully shove in one pine segment after another.

At these kilns, like the kilns of Bible history, the potters do not use thermometers or *cones;* they judge the temperature by the color inside the kiln. It is an exacting and demanding work. The pieces of pine for stoking a Mashiko kiln are usually cut and left to season no longer than two years lest the natural oils dry out. The stoker increases the heat intensity slowly and very gradually so that the pots will not crack from sudden changes in temperature.

I have seen the master potter himself come out in the rain and peek into the kiln when the flames were blazing at their peak and lapping at the sides of his pots. I have seen the stoker take a pair of iron tongs and skillfully *draw* out a sample *shard* and take it to the potter so he could judge the progress of a new or special glaze and give instructions for the next step.

When the kiln reaches the desired temperature, the stokers carefully cool down the chambers. Again, the cooling off process is slow and gradual. The potter knows that if he rushes the process, if he takes the pots out of the fire too soon, they will crack from the changes in temperature.

How like our God, who knows just how much of the fire we need, just how much adversity we can bear. God examines each of us individually, and on the basis of our whole person, He knows where to place us in the fire. His wisdom can determine whether we need to be sheltered by a previously fired vessel or whether we need the full heat of the fire.

Like the potter who attentively watches over the fire as it transforms his pots, God watches over us as we are going through our fire of affliction. And He says to us: "Fear not, for I have redeemed you; I have summoned you by name; you are mine. . . . When you walk through the fire, you will not be burned; the flames will not set you ablaze. For I am the LORD, your God, the Holy One of Israel, your Savior. . . . You are precious in my sight, . . . I love you. . . . Do not be afraid, for I am with you'" (Isaiah 43:1–5). He promises not only to be with us in the fire, but that the fire will not consume us. He knows when the fire has done its job. Only He knows the right time to pull us out of the fire.

When the vessels have expanded and contracted and cooled slowly enough, the chambers are unbricked and the pots are brought out to the potter. Only now, after this maturity firing and maturity cooling, can the potter enjoy a sort of fellowship with his creations. Before this they were too delicate, too touchy, too susceptible to damage inflicted by even the tenderest movement or the slightest breath.

Now there can be fellowship because the fire has done its work. In transforming the clay into pottery the fire has accomplished several purposes: it has burned away debris, hardened the pot, brought out the color, and matured it as a whole piece. The pot can be touched and moved about. It can enter into the life functions of a community. It has become that which the potter intended.

We are somewhere in the process of becoming what God intends. May God use our difficulties to transform us: to burn away the ugliness and unnecessary clutter, to strengthen us, to reveal our beauty, to mature us and help make us whole. And when the work of the fire is over, we will have complete fellowship with the Lord.

> "Blessed is the man who perseveres under trial, because when he has stood the test, he will receive the crown of life that God has promised for those who love him" (James 1:12).

Celebrating the Vessel

"He will take great delight in you" (Zephaniah 3:17).

The firing is finished. The last bundle of wood has been used to stoke the final chamber. For the greater part of two days and nights the fire has been manipulated from the lowest chamber to the highest, giving the longest heat to the pots stacked in the last chamber. Now workers fold up their blankets and stack them on a few remaining chunks of pine. The air is filled with a mixture of mystery and fatigue as they slowly bustle about to sweep up the dirt and make the ground neat around the kiln.

Tired bodies stretch and bend as if getting up from a long night's sleep, when in fact there has been no more than a few minutes of dozing off. The workers could go home now and sleep in their own beds, but there is a general excitement and a reluctance to leave. It is hard to let go, even though the kiln will be left now and the final embers will die out allowing each chamber to cool off for a few days.

The workers amble to the potter's house. There, the table is set and, like a harvest banquet, filled with food. More food is constantly brought in, served in large bowls that the potter made several years ago, bowls that today might sell for a large sum of money. This is a special occasion. Special soup made from mountain potatoes and mushrooms is served. Various meats, vegetables of all kinds, fish, raw salads of every color, home-made jellies, fruit, and steaming rice are served in heaping portions along with the best wine in the house.

The Japanese potter's banquet is no less impressive than the Jewish celebrations of Bible days when the people feasted the birth of a child, the weaning of a child, a wedding, the dedication of a newly built house, sheep-shearing, the new moon, or the feast of the Passover, the feast of Pentecost, and the feast of Trumpets and Ingathering.

Following the potter's feast in the Far East today there are about two days of visiting old friends and reminiscing with the family—a rest period before the big day of the kiln opening. Then when the kiln has sufficiently cooled, there comes the most exciting celebration of all: the opening of the kiln, one chamber at a time. It is this day for which all the other work days so far have existed; it is toward this moment that all efforts, all toil, all excitement have been aimed.

The unloading of the kiln is not usually open to the public, but only to the potter's closest friends and selected guests. His most celebrated friends, though, are the pots as they come forth, adorned in their splendid array of colors and clothed with the texture of his own creation.

At a single kiln opening there might be three thousand pots, or from one kiln in Okinawa as many as ten thousand pots unloaded in a day. Yet there is something singularly superb in every clay vessel.

Like a baby coming head first from the mother's womb, each clay vessel is brought gently out of the hollow belly of earth that served as its kiln. The master potter thoroughly examines each vessel and places it among the new forms; he recognizes them all but sees them now in their new coats, mature and stable vessels, unlike the fragile and colorless forms they had been before the firing. The inner joy and oneness of the potter with his clay is like a father holding his newborn child, and that moment of ecstasy, that reaching of the height of expectation, belongs to the potter alone; yet he is honored by the quiet presence of his friends, for he has invited only those who will sense and know something of what he feels.

People who attend the opening of a potter's kiln come for one reason: to honor the potter. Their presence is a gesture of respect to honor him. The unloading of a kiln is neither frivolous nor loud; the serene manner of the potter, is reflected in the serenity of friends he has chosen to invite as well as in the serenity of the pots that stand to exalt him. When the guests see a pot with a glaze they particularly like, their quiet oohs and ahs are an honor to the potter. Their walking beside him and listening for his comments are an honor to him. Their silent sensitivity to his unspoken feelings is an honor to him.

There is a taut moment when the worker chisels an opening in the mud chamber door, and excitement is released when the pots can be seen waiting their turn to come out. When the first pots from each chamber are handed to the master potter, that moment of shared joy and release of tenseness are themselves an honor to the potter.

The day of the kiln opening is a day of great joy and gratification. The Bible likewise shows God, at times, rejoicing over us. "He will take great delight in you; . . . he will rejoice over you with singing," said the prophet (Zephaniah 3:17). To think that God the Almighty would sing because of some joy I brought Him! This thought helps me determine with Paul, "We make it our goal to please him" (2 Corinthians 5:9).

134

[2]

In the cool of the day after all his guests have gone, the master potter walks among his created vessels as they stand on the ground lining the hillside along the path to his house. He gestures as if about to talk to them. He tenderly picks up a slender pitcher and tests its handle for strength. He touches every piece once more and gives a gentle thump to hear each ring with solidness.

The potter speaks as he bends down to sit among the earthen vessels. "Even as I have labored to bring you this far, you must also labor. Each of you has unique work to do. You are no longer reluctant clay. You are worthy vessels."

Gingerly he picks up a tiny piece simple in shape, simple in design, simple in color, and holds it in his hands. "Never doubt your worth, never be ashamed of what you are, sitting here in the shadow of this water jug so tall and elegant. Little vial, you will be filled with expensive oil," he says as he looks insistently at the tiny piece he is holding in his hands.

"I delighted to make you," he continues, "and you stood your ground in the fiery kiln the same as any jug that looks bigger than you. Both of you are big in my eyes, for neither of you was anything from the start," he points with a finger as if instructing a child in his arms. "From the chaotic clay, formless but not flawless, I found you and brought you to my house, and now you are what you are because I am the potter. If the world dislikes you, then it dislikes me, for I have put you here," he smiles.

Not meaning to intrude nor to eavesdrop on the potter in this quiet moment alone with his creation, we nevertheless feel a pull to move closer, for something in us identifies with the clay.

With an upswing of one hand the potter instructs them all, so that even we can hear, as if he is speaking to us as well: "Go and serve," he instructs. "In service you will find your reason to be. Meaning will come to you in serving."

Reflecting on the suffering world about us, we suddenly remember hearing the potter's concept before. Jesus said it of Himself: "For even the Son of Man did not come to be served, but to serve, and to give his life as a ransom for many" (Mark 10:45). Is that part of what the prophet meant, too, when he wrote, "O Lord . . . we are the clay, you are the potter; we are all the work of your hand"?

As if the Master is speaking through him, the potter continues: "Some of you will serve behind the scenes, where only the master of the house knows where you are and what you are doing. Others of you will be out front, where the world might praise you. In quiet dignity your emptiness is your potential, and therein is the real beauty to be admired.

"You have been created with unique personalities and with talents. You have been chosen to be what you are. Be nothing less!"

The potter singles out one piece and addresses it with loving dignity. "Little cup with a crooked handle, you are you, and you need not compete with this cream pitcher to prove your worth. How silly would the cream pitcher look trying to serve a hot drink and spilling it over the sides. You will be what you were created to be, and that is all I require of you—but I require that much."

Then the potter looks up and sees us standing there. But to him we are not intruders. To him we are one with his clay vessels sitting on the hillside path. With a wide sweep of his hand he includes us and continues talking.

"You have been transformed. Now you must go and be filled." He pauses. "And when you are filled, you must be emptied and then filled again. For this cause you were created."

The potter shifts his sitting position and bends a twig in his hand. Looking out over all the pots and then back at me, he speaks quietly and reflectively. "You are not the same as you once were when I found you heaped among the formless and the unknown, resistant and mixed with debris and other impurities not seen by human eyes.

"Smelly and coarse, you were unmanageable and incapable of holding a shape," he notes with a smile in his voice. Rubbing his hands as if remembering the sharp thorns that pierced them as he gathered the clay, he adds quickly, "But that was then, and now is now.

"I chose you, and in the cleansing water I separated you; I put you through the *pug mill* and you came out whole. As clay vessels your oneness is not in what you are and what you do; your oneness is in the stuff of which you are all made. The soft slurry made you able to be tough, and the tough workouts on the kneading board made you able to be soft. There is your oneness.

"I stretched you before you had a name; I named you before you had a shape. I put my image in you, and with long-suffering I have waited for this day, when your exterior image has come into harmony with your inner being. My aim has been to unbind what was bound; and now from the miry clay you are free."

I ponder on the paradox of the potter's words, "from the miry clay you are free." Yet the clay vessels are still clay. While their substance remains, their quality improved. Like sinners in a sinful world, the human remains human as the earth remains earthy. But in the hands of God, who is our Master Potter, even the lowliest of us can be refined and exalted to a second chance to be more tomorrow than we were yesterday. From nothingness we are formed, and in that form we have the freedom to be.

"I know the clays that crack under stress," the potter continues, "the clays that cling to those im-

138

pure elements brought from the past, that resist authority and change.

"But you are the clay that endured; you are the clay that responded when I urged you to give up an old habit and replace it with a better way; you are the clay that rested when I called you to rest. I am well pleased," says the potter.

Standing, he walks again along the path where the pots are lined, nodding his head in approval of the vessels, among which we stand. They have come through the fire. All of them are strong and able now to hold on to the shape he gave them.

"Oh, but comprehend the vastness of what you are!" he urges with both hands outstretched. "As my servants in a hurting world, you are vastly important. You are worthy vessels.

"Therefore, go. Go into all the world and give water to those who thirst. Go into all levels of the world, go to the rich and to the poor, and be what I have empowered you to be."

The potter turns and looks down the winding path. And I hear his words as if they are being spoken right in my ear.

"When I said, 'Come and follow me,' you came. When you intruded into my plan for another, I said, 'What is that to you? Follow me.' And now I tell you to go. Go wherever I send you.

"For from a shapeless earth I gave you shape. And in an aimless world I give you aim.

"Be all that you are, my worthy vessels."

Notes

[1] M.R. DeHaan, M.D., *The Chemistry of the Blood* (Grand Rapids: Zondervan Publishing House, 1971), 152.

[2] Susan Peterson, *Shoji Hamada: A Potter's Way and Work* (New York: Kodansha International USA, Ltd., 1974), 38.

[3] Ibid., 39.

[4] Daniel Rhodes, *Clay and Glazes for the Potter* (Radnor: Chilton Book Company, 1973), 65.

[5] Sarah K. Bolton, *Lives of Poor Boys Who Became Famous* (New York: Thomas Y. Crowell, Company, Publishers, 1962).

[6] Rackham Holt, *George Washington Carver* (Garden City: Doubleday and Company, Inc., 1963), 240.

[7] Bernard Brun, *Private Lives of the Great Composers* (New York: Library Publishers, 1955), 222.

[8] Wallace Brockway and Herbert Weinstock, *Men of Music* (New York: Simon and Schuster, 1950), 78.

[9] Margaret J. Anderson, *Let's Talk about God* (Minneapolis: Bethany Fellowship, Inc., 1975), 49.

[10] C.S. Lewis, *The Problem of Pain* (Glasgow: William Collins Sons Inc., 1940), 77.

[11] Arthur Sherburne Hardy, *Life and Letters of Joseph Hardy Neesima* (Boston: Houghton, Mifflin and Company, 1891), 9.

[12] Ibid., 338–339.

[13] Ibid., 31.

Glossary

Biscuit or bisque A clay object that has been shaped, air-dried, and fired once, without glaze, to produce a piece strong enough for decorating.

Bisque firing Preliminary low-temperature firing before glazing and subsequent firing at a higher temperature.

Blowhole A small opening at the top of a kiln to let out heat and facilitate cooling or to let out steam during the early part of firing.

Bung The term as used in this book refers to the lump of clay weighing approximately six pounds that has been neatly wedged for the last time and is ready to be put on the potter's wheel for centering and forming.

Clam To mud-in the door of a kiln.

Clay A decomposed, granite-type rock. To be classed as clay the decomposed rock must have fine particles so that it will be plastic. Clays should be free of vegetable matter but will often contain other impurities that affect their color and firing temperatures.

Collaring the clay To force the clay cylinder into a narrow shape as the neck of a vase or other vessel being formed while the wheel is in motion.

Cone A slender, unfired pyramid that softens and bends when sufficient heat and time have affected its composition. Used in modern kilns to indicate maturity point of the kiln load.

Dipping Glazing pottery by immersing it in a large pan or vat of glaze.

Draw To remove fired ware from the kiln.

Feldspar A rock containing oxides of silicon, aluminum, sodium potassium, and calcium. Used in clays and glazes.

Firing Applying sufficient heat for a necessary length of time to promote chemical change and elimination of all water from clay or glaze, thereby causing permanent hardening. *Bisque firing* makes air-dried greenware more durable and easier to decorate. *Glaze firing* causes chemical changes in glazes and other finishes on bisqueware and bonds them to the ware. Glazes have a different texture and color after firing. Temperature and time required in firing depend on the type of clay or glaze used and on the conditions of the kiln.

Flaking or scaling of slips and glazes during drying or firing. This usually results from uneven shrinkage or uneven drying, the body shrinking more than the glaze.

Glaze A coating of liquid-based glass which melts when heated and bonds to the clay surface. May be glossy, eggshell, matte, or textured, depending on the formula and the firing technique.

Glaze fire A firing cycle to the temperature at which the glaze materials will melt to form a glasslike surface coating. This is usually at the point of maximum body maturity and it is considerably hotter than the first bisque firing.

Greenware Pottery that has not been bisque fired.

Grog Ground up clay that has been fired, used in powder form to add porosity, texture, and strength to clay bodies.

Kiln The potter's furnace or oven capable of controlled temperature in which clay objects become pottery.

Kneading Working clay with the fingers or with the heel of the hand to make it into a uniform consistency.

Leather-hard Clay which is dried enough to be stiff, but which is still damp enough to be joined to other pieces with a slip (such as a handle added on) or to be carved. It holds its shape but is not chalk-hard as in greenware.

Maturity The optimum temperature for firing a clay or glaze to a tight, hard, serviceable structure, when the glaze ingredients enter into complete fusion, developing a strong bond with the body. After the maturity firing there is a pleasant surface texture and a maximum resistance to abrasion.

Ochres Natural iron earths, may be used as slips or as coloring pigments, generally turning to a moderate yellow.

Plasticity The quality of clay which allows it to be manipulated and still maintain its shape without cracking or sagging.

Porosity The state of being porous or able to pass liquids through the pores.

Potter's wheel The revolving wheel on which clay is shaped by hand. The wheel is either foot-powered or motor-driven, or in certain Asian potteries the wheel is hand-powered with a special stick.

Pug mill A machine which works much like a meat grinder to mix clay in its plastic state.

Primary clay Clay which has not been carried away by streams but has been found near the rock from which it was derived.

Raw clay Clay found in nature, not blended with other clay bodies.

Raw ware Ware that has been shaped and dried, but has not been fired. Greenware.

Refractory Resistant to heat.

Rib A tool of wood, bone, or metal, which is held in the potter's hand while throwing to assist in shaping the pot or to compact the clay.

Secondary clay Clays washed by nature from their source and settled in the quiet water of lakes and estuaries.

Shard A broken fragment of pottery.

Shrinkage The diminishing of the size of a clay piece due to water evaporation during air drying or chemical changes during firing. This normally ranges from 10% to 25%, depending on the kind of clay. Secondary clay shrinks more than primary clay.

Silica Oxide of silicone, SiO_2 found abundantly in nature as quartz, sandstone, flint, etc., and as a constituent of feldspar and clay.

Slip A clay in liquid form.

Slurry A creamy mixture of water and clay, often designating a thick clay slip or an unsieved slip.

Spiral screw An unwanted attitude of the clay on the potter's wheel. Unmanageable clay going off in an inverted screw shape that develops from trying to pull the clay from the middle of the hump rather than from the base. When the potter cups his hands around the clay spinning on the wheel and pulls it into a cone or cylinder, the spiraling effect causes the clay to wobble off center and become lopsided, and it must be pushed down and started over.

Stacking Loading a kiln for firing.

Throwing The operation of forming pieces on the potter's wheel from a plastic clay.

Vitrify To fire to the point of glassification.

Ware In general, pottery or porcelain in either the raw, bisque, or glazed state.

Warping Clay ware losing its shape (curling, twisting, distorting) due to improper drying or firing. Uneven walls can especially cause warping unless the pieces are dried extra carefully.

Weathering The exposure of raw clay to the action of rain, sun, and freezing weather which breaks down the particle size and makes clay more plastic.

Wedging Kneading and cutting plastic clay, forcibly throwing down one piece on the other to cause a uniform texture free from air pockets.